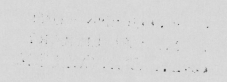

TEXAS HILL COUNTRY

Text and Photographs by
GEORGE OXFORD MILLER

Voyageur Press

Other books by George Miller
Texas Parks and Campgrounds
Texas Photo Safaris
A Field Guide to Wildlife of Texas and the Southwest
A Field Guide to Wildflowers, Trees, and Shrubs of Texas
and
Landscaping with Native Plants of Texas and the Southwest

Printed in Singapore

91 92 93 94 95   5 4 3 2 1

Library of Congress Cataloging-in-Publication Data

Miller, George Oxford, 1943–
Texas Hill Country / George O. Miller.
    p.   cm.
ISBN 0-89658-164-0
1. Natural history—Texas—Texas Hill Country. 2. Texas Hill Country (Tex.)—Description and travel. 3. Texas Hill Country (Tex.)—Social life and customs. I. Title.
QH105.T4M55 1991
508.764—dc20   91-13082
                                                                          CIP

Published by
Voyageur Press, Inc.
P.O. Box 338, 123 North Second Street
Stillwater, MN 55082 U.S.A.
From Minnesota and Canada 612-430-2210
Toll-free 800-888-9653

Voyageur Press books are also available at discounts for quantities for educational, fundraising, premium, or sales-promotion use. For details contact the marketing department. Please write or call for our free catalog of natural history publications.

On page 5: Baháí statement from *The Baháí Statement on Nature*, Baháí International Community Office of Public Information, 866 United Nations Plaza, Suite 120, New York, NY 10017.

CONTENTS

AUTUMN LEAVES IN LOST MAPLES
STATE NATURAL AREA

*"The country is the world of the soul, the city
is the world of bodies."*

*"Nature in its essence is the embodiment of My Name, the
Maker, the Creator. . . . Nature is God's Will and is its
expression in and through the contingent world."*
Baha'u'llah, The Baha'i Statement on Nature

INDIAN PAINTBRUSH (*CASTILLEJA INDIVISA*)
IN TRAVIS COUNTY

A CALL FROM CASTELL

"The land retains an identity of its own,
still deeper and more subtle than we can know. Our
obligation toward it then becomes simple: to approach with
an uncalculating mind, with an attitude of regard . . . and
to be alert for its openings, for that moment when something
sacred reveals itself within the mundane, and you know the
land knows you are there."
Barry Lopez, Arctic Dreams

Don't look for Castell on your Rand McNally map. It barely appears on the official Texas highway map. It's just a white dot on a gray line, the lowliest designations for both a town and a paved road. The map index generously gives the hamlet a population of seventy-two. I was just passing through Castell, tarrying from one sunset to the next sunrise, in search of the perfect field of bluebonnets. But in this dot-on-the-map town, I discovered more than flowers.

Castell is located in the scenic Hill Country, the heart of Texas both geographically and metaphorically. The Hill Country, with its poor-in-soil terrain and scarce-in-rain weather, frustrates farmers, inspires photographers and painters, and gratifies ranchers with its abundant gift of grass. Texans link the romantic image of the cowboy and cattle drive with these rugged hills.

In the spring, the craggy granite hills around Castell abound with dainty wildflowers. Bluebonnets, paintbrushes, phlox, daisies, and wine cups blanket the roadsides and fields like a multicolored quilt. Most of the wildflower pictures that decorate Texas calenders come from this region. Every town large enough to have a chamber of commerce, which excludes Castell, sponsors bluebonnet trails, festivals, and art shows.

I drove into Castell just as the long afternoon shadows began chasing the bewitching light of dusk across the countryside. I abruptly braked and pulled off the road. I cut the engine, opened the door, and stepped out. (Here you don't feel compelled to shut the door.) In front of me, isolated on the curbless street, illuminated by a lonely street light, was a red and white phone booth, a relic of a bygone era.

The scene resembed a Salvador Dali landscape. Grass crept over the edge of the square cement floor and a vine twisted its way through a ventilation louver in the base. The booth beckoned me in some magical way to step inside and shut the door. I fantasized that I could deposit a quarter, dial a number, and instantly be swept away to some starry destination.

Impulsively I stepped into the booth and pulled the door shut. I checked the vine to be sure it wasn't about to coil around my leg. A dime lay on the dusty floor. How long had it been there? Since a phone call cost ten cents? I looked at the phone, trying to decide whom to call. Then a thought made me quiver: What if it suddenly rang and a strange voice asked for me?

Across the street from the phone booth was the Castell General Store. A sheet of paper on the front door apologized "Sorry, Closed Early Today." Snuggled against one end of the whitewashed structure leaned a one-room post office with a dozen or so boxes visible through the window. A lifeless flag hung from the regulation pole common to every federal building, regardless of size. The store proprietor had chalked a happy face and "Welcome Home Kelly" greeting on a slate message board above a bench on the porch.

I imagined the bustle of activity around the steps and front porch of the store during the day. The social and business life of the town probably centered around the two unpainted benches on either side of the front door. Friends met there, exchanged gossip, sold cattle, hired workers, and sealed agreements with a handshake. But at this late hour, only a black cat with its head tucked between its white paws occupied one of the benches.

A cactus wren landed on the wire above the booth and briefly interrupted the tranquil evening with is throaty *hut-hut-hut-hut*. Then, as twilight settled over the town, bats began spilling from underneath the roof of the store. They tumbled down like children rolling off the upper bunk and swooped low over the phone booth before gaining altitude.

Here I am, I thought, alone at dusk in a red-and-white phone booth, dodging bats and squeezing a quarter in my left hand. Do I really want to make contact with the outside world? I put the quarter in my pocket, stepped out of the booth, and listened to the evening sounds echoing across the countryside.

I spent the night on a side road under a windmill that groaned in the breeze like a demented spirit. At first light, I drove back into Castell. Four black cows were grazing in a field at the edge of town. They wandered through the morning mist like shadowy apparitions. With tripod-mounted camera, I waited for the sun's first rays to splash vitalizing light across the scene of flowers, phantomlike cattle, and background steeple.

The morning had begun for most folks an hour or so earlier. Pickup trucks rattled by on the narrow two-lane, farm-to-market road in an abbreviated version of rush-hour traffic. After three or four trucks passed, the bumpy roadway regained its tranquility. The sky began turning kitchen cabinet yellow, promising the sun's appearance at any minute. The cows chose that moment to make their retreat to some unseen barn, leaving the foreground embarrassingly vacant for the photograph I had visualized. I quickly folded my tripod and retreated a few blocks to a low-water crossing over the Llano River, hoping to catch the sun rising over the water.

The Llano ran wide and shallow, slightly swollen from recent showers. Too low to inundate the roadway, the water poured through culverts, creating twin channels in the rocky bed. Black silhouettes of willows, sycamores, and buttonbushes loomed against the skyline. Finally, the sun peaked over the horizon, first like a timid schoolgirl, then faster, like a ballerina trailing her crimson gown across the water's placid surface. Moments later, the sky lost its blush and the day officially began.

The sun, its orb fully outlined in the sky, wasted no time in vanquishing the ephemeral mist hovering above the river. On this spring morning, the air still had an exhilarating nip. In another month, the hot breath of summer would smother the delicate crispness of dawn.

The invigorating air of the Hill Country is a treasure lost in the asphalt avenues of cities. Its night air cradles the stars just beyond reach. You can drink its morning air like a tonic—a heady brew that alters time and beckons you to stop at a crossroads cafe for a cup of coffee. Its unsullied air doesn't sting your eyes or bite your nose, or carry a load of fumes like a wandering garbage truck.

On this morning the gentle breeze touched the bluebonnets blanketing the roadsides and spread their perfume across the fields like good news. And like the bees diving in and out of the blossoms, I felt the seductive lure of the aroma, inviting me and my camera for a more intimate investigation.

Fields of flowers unblemished by footprints, air unadulterated with human additives, stars undimmed by city lights, and the uninterrupted sounds of nature—this is what I found in Castell. Experiencing the beauty and purity of nature inspires the human spirit. It clarifies our values. It reminds us of the true ingredients of happiness. Encountering the creative force in nature sparks the creative force within. We respond with art and poetry, with praise and gratitude. I left Castell feeling a renewal of life and a oneness with all creation. I felt an extravagant pleasure in being alive. I had received an unexpected wake-up call in this sleepy little town.

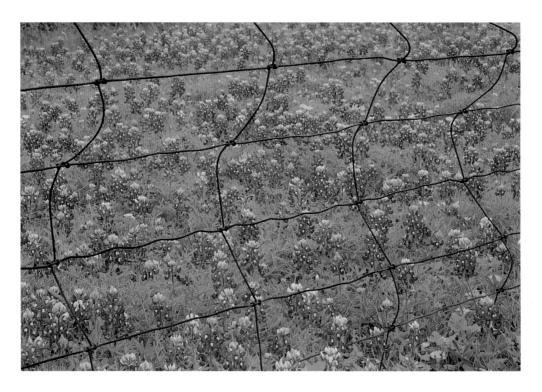

BLUEBONNETS (*LUPINUS TEXENSIS*) AND
A WEATHERED FENCE IN HAYS COUNTY

SUNRISE AT THE LLANO RIVER IN CASTELL

A SPLIT IN THE ROAD, GILLESPIE COUNTY

REFLECTIONS AT THE WESTCAVE PRESERVE, TRAVIS COUNTY

A TEXAS SUN SETS AGAINST A WINDMILL

THE MYSTIQUE OF THE HILLS

"200 miles to the nearest post office
100 miles to wood
20 miles to water
6 inches to hell
God bless our home."
Inscription on an early settler's log cabin in Blanco
County, from Rose Hauk, Hearts Home

What constitutes a "promised land?" I can think of two historical examples of a people searching for and finding an actual place: Israel for the Jews and the southwestern mesas for the Hopi. In each case, the land indelibly influenced the society, created legends, became interwoven with the people's spiritual and cultural identity, and enabled the people to survive for millennia.

According to legend, the Hopis migrated from west to east across the American continent and from the Arctic wastes to the tip of Argentina and back again, looking for their promised land. They settled in areas rich in natural resources, but found that riches and ease made them vulnerable. When their society crumbled around them as a result of moral lassitude, they knew it was time to move on. Finally, they reached the desert mesas of the southwestern United States. They could survive on this land's meager resources, but not grow fat. They realized one of nature's immutable laws: Only the lean and hard survives, whether it be a microbe, a human, or a culture.

Some ten years ago, I visited Israel. I looked out across the overgrazed limestone hills surrounding Jerusalem and saw stunted trees and bare stone reflecting the torrid Mediterranean sun. I was ten thousand miles from Texas, yet if I blinked I would think I was back in the Hill Country. Deep inside I realized why the Jewish people loved this desolate country.

You love a promised land not for what it gives you but for what it demands of you. It demands the very quality that makes humans proud to be alive: a strong character that refuses to give up in the face of seemingly insurmountable obstacles.

The promised lands throughout history have been countries that sustained and nourished, but at a price. The price was sacrifice, but the reward was survival, the ultimate payoff both physical and spiritual. Nature has no patience with the slothful indulgence engendered by overabundance. We humans may dream of utopias flowing with milk and honey, but our legends, our mythical prototypes, come from those who wrested their livelihood from a hostile environment.

The Texas Hill Country meets all the historical and traditional requirements of a promised land. It was settled on a promise, though one defaulted. In the 1840s, the Society for the Protection of German Immigrants, a group of German nobles, promised settlers a section of rich farmland between the Colorado and Llano rivers. Because of Indian hostilities, the uprooted Germans had to settle for the more rugged, hilly country between New Braunfels and Fredericksburg.

Claiming a promised land has never been easy. The German immigrants had to wrestle the land from the previous inhabitants. They discovered that they were invading the territory of the fiercest, most hostile Indians in North America, the Comanche. The Comanche, who had been pushed out of the Central Plains by white settlers, had already deposed the Tonkawas and displaced the infamous Apaches. Understandably, they were not kindly disposed to another wave of white settlers surging across their land. Stories of Indian raids, kidnappings, massacres, and finally a peace treaty still celebrated in Fredericksburg flavor the Hill Country's history.

As with other promised lands, the Hill Country is roofed with broad skies and billowing clouds, carpeted with rocky soil, and seasoned with soaring summer temperatures. It has just enough soil and receives just enough rain to tempt its inhabitants. Success is possible, but it is a challenge. It's a hard land, land that tests the worth of its people. A prophet from another promised land once said, "With fire we test the gold." The gold of the Hill Country is the people it forges with the flames of hardship.

The marginal quality of the Hill Country tempers the characters of those who depend on it for a livelihood. It is also responsible for this region's charm and appeal today. The Hill Country is both geographically and metaphorically located in the heart of Texas. The romantic image of the hardened pioneer who faced the challenge head-on and conquered the land is the heart, the spirit, the essence of the image of Texans. And nowhere is the image better exemplified than in the rugged Hill Country.

Nature and geography have joined forces to keep the population of the Hill Country to a minimum. Most of its thin soil is too rocky to plow, droughts periodically assault the land, and much better grasslands exist to the north, south, and east. As Texas cities double and triple in size, the wide open spaces of the Hill Country become even more romantic and desirable.

People from the burgeoning metropolitan complexes are spilling out of the cities like a Kerr County flash flood. The retired and weekend residents of the Hill Country don't have to wrench survival from the land. They can sit back and enjoy the view, a luxury those depending on a ranching economy seldom can afford. As blue as the Mediterranean, impounded reservoirs now lap at the rocky shorelines of the cedar-covered hills. Water skiers cut across scarlet sunsets, and vacation homes sit perched on hilltop over-

14

looks. No, the struggle for survival today is not the same as it was one hundred, or even fifty or twenty-five years ago.

A rapid change in inhabitants and culture is nothing new for the Hill Country. Born of fire and water, shaped by rain and wind, and sculpted by the voracious appetites of cows, sheep, and goats, this country has lived through countless cycles of comings and goings. It has seen dinosaurs come and go, Indians come and go, cowboys come and go, and tall grass come and go. The hills now see mesquites and cedars, goats and sheep, exotic animals, dams and lakes, and recreation homes coming. But the rugged hills have a timeless quality, a changeless nature in which change is measured not in human life-times, but in millions of years.

Maybe the permanence of the Hill Country is the root of its appeal to modern humans, for on a subconscious level we thirst for stability in our lives, something we can depend on, some places where we can sink our spiritual and physical roots. Nothing satisfies as much as stepping out on your porch and seeing a view that you know your grandchildren will enjoy as much as you do now. Only time will tell if the Hill Country will become a crowded suburb of retirees and wealthy refugees from the city. Let's hope it doesn't.

LOST MAPLES STATE NATURAL AREA

WILDFLOWERS IN HAYS COUNTY

HAMILTON CREEK IN TRAVIS COUNTY

BIGTOOTH MAPLE
(*ACER GRANDIDENTATUM*) LEAVES

HAMILTON POOL IN TRAVIS COUNTY

BORN OF FIRE AND WATER

"A soil that cannot be plowed under keeps it
traditions—and its secrets."
J. Frank Dobie, Coronado's Children

The rugged hills in the heart of Texas were born of fire and water, the basic elements that Aristotle used to represent continual conflict. Like a detective, a trained observer can decipher the ageless turmoil in the twisted, melted, and worn rock strata. A casual traveler cannot help but see and feel, and perhaps marvel at, the results of the eternal conflict. You see the first evidence of it just west of Interstate 35 between Georgetown and San Antonio. A low range of hills juts out of the blackland prairie. The deep scars from rock quarry strip mines reveal that Texas has a heart of stone—limestone.

This juncture of flat prairie and rugged limestone hills results from one of the most important geological features in Texas, the Balcones Fault. The upper side of the fault stretches like a spread-out horseshoe from Del Rio to San Antonio and curves north through Austin. It disappears underground near Temple. Within the open semicircle of the fault line, nature's cycle of deposition and erosion has sculpted the Edwards Plateau into the rugged Hill Country. At the edge of the fault, hills rise out of the prairie sod and great springs gush crystal-pure water at a rate of millions of gallons per day. Humans have lived near the springs at Del Rio, San Antonio, New Braunfels, San Marcos, and Austin for thirty thousand years.

Few of us stop to contemplate that events that transpired millions of years ago dictate our profession, recreation, and culture. But by supplying water, soil, and minerals, the lay of the land directs the society it sustains. The essence of the Hill Country as we know it today—its resources, its character, its charm—is inherited from its geological past, the series of events that began sometime back in geological time (that means so long ago that it boggles our minds) and stretches through today and into the unforeseen future.

As you climb west onto the Edwards Plateau, say on Texas 71 or U.S. 290, you are traveling backward through geological time. You can time-travel back 135 million years and find dinosaur tracks in the flat rock bottoms of the Blanco and San Gabriel rivers. Step back three hundred million years at Pedernales Falls State Park and discover crinoids in the rock strata along the river. But don't stop yet. At the San Saba River bridge south of Brady, you can journey back six hundred million years and see fossils of some of the earliest known life forms, sea algae resembling two-foot lily pads. The road into the past continues beyond the emergence of life to a time when the earth was in its infancy. The Valley Spring Gneiss at Inks Lake State Park dates back one billion years. The pinkish crystals of feldspar were formed deep within the earth in rocks subjected to intense heat and pressure, and exposed to modern eyes by uplift and erosion.

So the roots of the Hill Country date back to primordial time when the continents were just forming. Since then, nature's cycle of deposition and erosion has shaped and reshaped this area countless times. During the Cambrian era, five to six hundred million years ago, shallow seas covered central Texas and deposited thick sediments of limestone, shale, and marine sandstone. Then the seas receded and erosion began wearing away the solidified sediments. The cycle was repeated about 450 million years ago, and Ordovician seas laid down 1,400 feet of limestone known today as the Ellenburger group. Geologists find shallow sea deposits from 350 million, three hundred million, and eighty-five million years ago. During the late Cretaceous period, about seventy-five million years ago, a great uplift began pushing the coastline hundreds of miles to the east and exposing an eastward-sloping plateau of sedimentary rock thousands of feet thick. Just as life itself once had, the Edwards Plateau emerged from the sea. In moist periods, such as the ice ages, rivers ran deep and wide and cut steep valleys. During the brief interval of geological time since the plateau's emergence, rain and wind have sculpted the hills we see today. A look at the level horizon reveals that this rugged terrain was carved from a flat slab of limestone.

MOUNTAINS OF MAGMA

North of Burnet, FM 2341 winds through the heart of a unique area called the Central Texas Mineral Region, or the Llano Uplift. Though glaring white limestone hills characterize most of the Edwards Plateau, the hills surrounding Fredericksburg, Llano, and Burnet are distinctively different. They glow red and pink in the setting sun, for they were born not of water, but of fire. About one billion years ago an enormous upwelling of molten rock cooled deep underground, forming an immense mass of granite known as a batholith. The heat and pressure from the magma intrusion metamorphosed the surrounding rocks into gneiss and schist. The last uplift exposed the overlying strata of solidified sea sediments, and the cycle shifted again from deposition to erosion.

The narrow blacktop road passes what was once the largest graphite mine in North America, an abandoned lead mine, an ancient travertine waterfall (usually dry), and the shores of Lake Buchanan. The road curves around a hill overlooking the lake and colorful cake layers of green clay in the road cut come into view. I remember my geology professor telling field trip students to taste the strange green clay. We all dutifully followed his instructions and put a pinch in our mouths. We looked at each other inquisitively. It tasted just like dirt. Then, with a chuckle, the teacher informed us that we had just tasted petrified fish feces.

Millions of years of rain and wind stripped away thousands of feet of overlying strata to expose the granite and metamorphic bedrock. The crystalline structure of the heat-tempered rocks caused them to weather into the coarse sand that covers the hills and forms the sandy banks of streams and rivers that flow through the region. Numerous exposed granite mountains and domes dot the area, but two have special significance, Enchanted Rock and Granite Mountain.

Rising 445 feet above the surrounding terrain, the symmetrical dome of Enchanted Rock resembles a giant red onion arching above the horizon. Geologically, it is called an exfoliation dome, and as such it is second in size in the United States to Stone Mountain in Georgia. The dome itself is but a small knob on the southern end of the batholith. Fifty million years of uplift and erosion exhumed Enchanted Rock from deep within the earth. Like a balloon taken from low to high altitude, the massive batholith began to expand ever so slightly as the pressure from the overlying rocks diminished. Weathering caused cracks and joints in the exposed sections of the batholith and, like a jeweler's chisel, erosion cut out diamond-shaped mountains. The release of internal pressure caused the outer surface to split and peel away in onionskin layers, giving the mountains a domed profile. The exfoliation sheets are clearly visible on Enchanted Rock, varying from a few inches to many yards in thickness. Realizing the geological, ecological, and historical significance of the rock, the Texas Nature Conservancy purchased 1,643 acres and transferred the site to the state in 1978 to be operated as a state natural area.

Enchanted Rock is composed of Town Mountain granite, renowned for its striking pink color. Were it not for its coarse composition, this famous landmark might have suffered the same fate as Granite Mountain in Marble Falls and Bear Mountain near Fredericksburg. The pink color of the granite has placed it in high demand for a hundred years. In 1885, land developers, looking for a way to draw people to the newly founded town of Marble Falls, offered to donate granite for the proposed state capitol building. The state used convict labor to build a railroad spur from Marble Falls to Burnet to haul the stone chiseled from Granite Mountain to Austin. The quarry is still chipping away at the mountain. The shaped and polished granite slabs decorate skyscrapers reaching toward the heavens and graves commemorating the dead.

DREAMS AND SCHEMES

While small-town cafes and bars in west Texas entertained conversations of cattle and grass, customers at turn-of-the-century establishments in Llano and Burnet talked of mining fortunes. The Central Texas Mineral Region is rich in variety of minerals, more so than in volume. The slow cooling of the batholith deep in the bosom of the earth allowed minerals to crystallize. Llano County boasts that 241 minerals can be found within its environs. Molybdenum, tungsten, fluorspar, gypsum, iron, lead, asbestos, bismuth, copper, feldspar, chromium, and manganese are just a few of the materials that excited prospectors and investors.

Most of the mining ventures generated more excitement than profit, except for the shysters with lucrative, get-rich-quick schemes. However, some mines were remarkably successful. The world's largest graphite mine operated for decades north of Burnet. A small hill, now inundated by Lake Buchanan, yielded green ore composed of precious rare earth elements. In 1887, yttrium brought $144 per ounce, but the boom was short-lived. The mineral's value depended on its content of gadolinite, a necessary ingredient for preincandescent lamps, and the only other source was Russia. By 1904, the incandescent lamp with a wire filament was widespread, and the mine closed down. A lead mine west of Burnet yielded only twenty-nine tons of the metal before closing in 1930.

While lead, iron, rare earth minerals, and ferroalloys attracted attention and some commercial interest, gold and silver fired the imagination of the early settlers and later prospectors. Various historical accounts abound with legends of rich veins of gold and silver. Texas author J. Frank Dobie documents many of the stories in his book *Coronado's Children*. The Apache and Comanche gathered nuggets off the floor or chipped them off the walls of a mine on Packsaddle Mountain. Other mines reportedly exist near the confluence of Honey Creek and the San Saba, along the headwaters of the Frio River, and near Enchanted Rock. The Indians or Spaniards apparently always filled in and concealed the mines before abandoning them, and did such a good job that the mines have remained undiscovered.

The cloak of mystery still shrouds the hills of central Texas, as much today as in times past. Geologists comb the hills for clues to its violent past. Modern treasure seekers still dream of hidden wealth. Once on the side of a rocky hill I found half of a spear point resting on a tiny pedestal of dirt. The rain had washed away the surrounding soil and left it uncovered, glinting in the sun. Wonder filled me as I stood looking at the sculpted chip of rock. What had happened here? How had the spear point been broken? In an animal, in a human? Finally, I reached down and pocketed this clue from the past. The hills hold many secrets—secrets they will never reveal.

THE NATURAL BRIDGE CAVERNS IN COMAL COUNTY

THE HEADWATERS OF THE FRIO RIVER IN REAL COUNTY

PURSLANE (*PORTULACA* SPECIES), AN AUTUMN FLOWER,
IN ENCHANTED ROCK STATE NATURAL AREA

MCKINNEY FALLS, MCKINNEY FALLS STATE PARK

WHITE ROCK WATERFALL NEAR BURNET

ROCK PATTERNS AT PEDERNALES FALLS STATE PARK

THE MEDINA RIVER

RIVERS OF LIFE

"Once in a lifetime, if one is lucky, one so merges
with the sunlight and air and running water that whole
eons, the eons that mountains and deserts know,
might pass in a single afternoon without discomfort."
Loren Eiseley, The Immense Journey

The wind, warmed by the sun and propelled by barometric pressures, sweeps across the Gulf of Mexico, sucking up its moisture. Imagine a drop of water riding the foamy crest of a wind-driven whitecap until, unable to resist the airy Siren's call, it abandons its liquid body and becomes one with the breeze. Bloated with water vapor, the airborn "high tide" races inland, leaving the rolling surf lapping at the shoreline.

Deflected upward at landfall, the wind, satiated from its banquet in the warm Gulf, carries our vaporous drop thousands of feet above its watery home. The drop's journey takes it inland over flat prairies and scattered woodlands. Geologically speaking, this featureless plain was only recently resurrected from the ocean floor. After about 125 miles of unimpeded westward flight, the wind encounters an obstacle: the Edwards Plateau. This eastward-dipping wall of rock rises out of the blackland prairie like a stony sentinel demanding tribute from all that blows over its sunbaked surface. The wind resists, clinging to its treasure of moisture. But like a Barbary pirate, the heat rising off the limestone hills exacts its payment. The rising thermals force the moisture-laden sea breeze high into the atmosphere. As the coastal air cools, it loses its appetite for moisture. Now thousands of feet in elevation and hundreds of miles inland, our drop once again regains its liquid composition and begins its journey back to the sea.

This confluence of moisture-rich air and thermals rising over the Hill Country creates some of the most turbulent thunderstorms in the nation. On average, more than fifty thunderstorms a year strike the Hill Country, some producing updrafts exceeding 6,000 feet per minute (seventy miler per hour). The greatest rainstorm in U.S. history occurred along the eastern edge of the Edwards Plateau in 1921. The community of Thrall received 36.4 inches of rain in eighteen hours. In 1952, twenty-six inches of rain pelted the Kerrville area in one day. The Pedernales River rose above the arching canopy of cypress trees lining its picturesque banks and stripped the shoreline clean.

Though rampaging at flood stage, Hill Country rivers normally set a leisurely pace in their portage of rainwater to the sea. The names themselves—Medina, Frio, Sabinal, Blanco, Guadalupe—have a beguiling ring reminiscent of lazy summer afternoons and blue-cold swimming holes. The base flow for these romantic streams comes from water hidden underground in a vast reservoir of porous, fractured limestone called the Edwards Aquifer. The character of the Hill Country is molded as much by this underground aquifer as it is by its rugged hills and starry nights.

In the marvelous scheme of nature, our errant raindrop normally would not rush wantonly down some steep hillside to join streams and rivers in a common quest for the sea. No, accepting the hospitality of the thirsty hills, the watery traveler soaks in and stays for a while, maybe decades, maybe centuries. But the time comes when the march to the sea cannot be delayed, and our drop escapes its underground labyrinth.

About one hundred million years ago, a process began deep within the earth that predetermined life on the land today. The massive plate carrying the North American continent like a giant turtle collided with other plates and warped. During that cataclysmic period of mountain formation and volcanic eruptions, the Texas coastline coincided closely with the present route of Interstate 35 from Dallas to San Antonio. During the last seventy-five million years, the seas receded and the Edwards Plateau pushed upward. Its present tilt from 2,700 feet in the west to 750 feet at its eastern edge drains the water hidden in its porous heart eastward. The water flows underground until it reaches the upside of the Balcones Fault Zone, which exposes the water-bearing strata.

Flowing springs and dripping seeps create watery veins of life coursing through the rocky hills of central Texas. Like an unfailing heart, the aquifers have pumped life-sustaining water for countless millennia. Some of the largest springs in the Southwest occur along the Balcones Fault Zone in Del Rio (San Felipe Springs), Brackettville, Uvalde (Leona Springs), San Antonio, New Braunfels (Comal Springs), San Marcos, and Austin (Barton Springs). The San Marcos Springs pour out more than one hundred million gallons of sparkling water daily. Archaeological evidence indicates the springs have attracted humans to the rocky hillside of their emergence for twelve thousand years, making this one of the oldest continually inhabited localities in North America.

The constancy and purity of water has allowed plant and animal species to evolve that live in the San Marcos River and nowhere else in the world. This unique river has the highest concentration of endangered species in the nation. The first three miles of crystal flowing water harbor the last few colonies of Texas wild rice and the only populations of two small fish, the San Marcos gambusia, possibly already extinct, and the fountain darter. The San Marcos salamander survives in the headwaters of the springs. Several other large spring systems host their own unique species of salamanders and aquatic life. More bizarre yet are the creatures that live within the confines of the aquifer itself. The eyeless, lungless Texas blind salamander, the first animal placed on the endangered species list, and two species of blindcat fish never see the light of day.

The Hill Country that so delights our senses today is different in several remarkable ways from the grass-covered hills where the Apache and Comanche roamed and later German, Hispanic, and Anglo settlers farmed and ranched. The grinding molars of cattle, sheep, and goats have literally reshaped the hills. For one hundred years, these grazing animals have methodically removed the protective layer of grass covering the chalky skeleton of the hills. Once exposed, the thin skin of soil cannot withstand the torrential downpours, and joins the rain in its march to the sea. Without a thick vegetative cover to slow the runoff of the rain, the water flows into the streams instead of soaking in and recharging the aquifers. With inadequate recharge, the future of these fountains of life is limited.

Once only windmills sipped the elixir of life from the porous depths of the Hill Country. Now cities, farms, and industries pump an average of 530,000 acre-feet per year from the San Antonio region of the aquifer. (One acre-foot equals one foot of water covering one acre, or 325,851 gallons.) Pumping more than 450,000 acre-feet per year threatens spring flow. All but the San Marcos Springs dried up during the drought that ended in 1956. After tens of thousands of years of constancy, the San Marcos Springs will greet the twenty-first century with an intermittent flow unless effective water-use management occurs.

Water has always been the dominant force in the Hill Country. Geologically, the Cretaceous seas laid down the limestone sediments that formed the Edwards Plateau. Climatically, rain and erosion carved the plateau into the rugged hills we see today. Ecologically, the springs and streams nourish the plant and animal life. Economically, the availability of water determines the livelihood of its residents and the location of its cities. Politically, whoever controls the water, controls the land.

The influence of water took on a new dimension in 1938 when Buchanan Dam began to tame the free-flowing, often rampaging, Colorado River. Before that time, the Colorado flooded Austin periodically, and had washed away the first dam that impounded Lake Austin. Soon other dams created a series of lakes realtors like to call a string of pearls on the Colorado. Inks Lake is just downstream from Lake Buchanan, followed by Lake Lyndon B. Johnson, Lake Marble Falls, Lake Travis, and Lake Austin. Town Lake in Austin is impounded by a low-water dam located where cowboys driving longhorns up the Chisolm Trail forded the river. The scenic Guadalupe River has one impoundment, Canyon Lake, just upstream from New Braunfels.

Through the years, the lakes have prevented millions of dollars of flood damage and provided recreation for millions of people, but taming the rivers has taken its toll on wildlife. Hill Country rivers feed the rich coastal estuaries and bays from Matagorda to Corpus Christi. The inland bays and lagunas support some of the most productive nursery grounds on the Gulf coast for fish, shrimp, and oysters. The multimillion-dollar fishing industry depends on healthy estuaries, yet the dams are holding back the life-giving fresh waters and nutrients. In times of drought when cities, farmers, and industry claim their surface water rights, the estuaries languish. In 1989, the whooping cranes returning to their wintering grounds in Arkansas National Wildlife Refuge found the marshes three times saltier than sea water.

The lakes themselves, though picturesque and nursing numerous resorts, are not in balance with the dynamic elements of the Hill Country. In years of drought, the water level drops drastically, leaving marinas, swimming beaches, and lakeside lots hundreds of feet from the refreshing blue waters. Worse yet, the dams impound more than the water carried by the rivers; they capture the silt. The fingerlike tributaries and rivers flowing into the lakes cling to their load of silt until the impoundment slows their flow. The sand and clay once held in place on the hills by the tenacious roots of grass now settle to the dark bottom of the artificial lake. Each year the lake bottom creeps upward toward the surface like a slow moving avalanche in reverse. More than forty feet of sediments have built up in Lake Buchanan, about ten inches per year. Town Lake, at the far end of the string of pearls, is largely silted in.

Today, the allure of the lakes beckons us with a call different from the one heard by early settlers. The pioneers seeking a new life encountered hostile Indians, unforgiving climate, and rugged terrain. For them the rocky hills represented hard work and, most likely, a shortened lifespan. Today, the rippling surface of the lakes reflecting the setting sun invites us with the promise of leisure and recreation. Seeking escape from hostile traffic, stressful jobs, and impatient landlords, we come to the hills. We come to savor a country still rooted in a time when the call of the wild woke us every morning.

The tailored lakeside communities with condos, golf courses, and marinas epitomize the role of water in the Hill Country. The wealth, the charm, the life of these hills exist in their water—in the crystal-pure springs and the rivers they nourish. Water is the essence of the Hill Country; take it away and all that remains is the arid reminder of a treasure squandered. The challenge of the pioneers was to survive war parties raiding their homes. The challenge facing us now is the antiquated laws that allow us to raid the underground aquifers until the pumps run dry.

San Antonio, one of the largest metropolitan areas in the nation, consumes 65 percent of the water from the southern region of the Edwards Aquifer. The average urbanite uses 180 gallons of water per day, and the population grows daily. As subdivisions creep westward into the Hill Country, the demand for water increases, creating an even greater imbalance between the recharge rate and the pumping output. People want their green lawns, whether in the city or country. Currently, 44 percent of urban water goes to watering thirsty landscapes, and as much as half of that is wasted through runoff.

Farmers and ranchers whose lives and livelihood depend on the aquifers have a dim view of this unbalance. Why should city people indulge their thirsty lawns and deprive the agricultural sector of water needed for crops and livestock? For the Hill Country to survive today, we must look beyond personal fence lines, beyond city jurisdiction, and beyond traditional codes of water ownership to establish meaningful laws that protect and preserve the underground water, the lifeblood, of the Hill Country.

CREEK AT INKS LAKE STATE PARK

KRAUSE SPRINGS IN BURNET COUNTY

SPRING ON THE PEDERNALES RIVER IN BLANCO COUNTY

THE SABINAL RIVER IN LOST MAPLES STATE NATURAL AREA

A JUVENILE RACCOON (*PROCYON LOTOR*)

MAMMALS BY THE MILLIONS

*"Most of the world's largest bat colonies are already
gone, and the few that remain are extremely vulnerable."
Dr. Merlin Tuttle, founder, Bat Conservation International,
from an article in* Defenders *magazine*

Water sprayed from under the tires as I drove across the low-water crossing of the Frio River. After fording the stream, I turned off the paved FM highway. My companion unlocked the rancher's gate with a borrowed key. The twin ruts wound through a rocky pasture and disappeared over a small but steep hill. The going was slow, but easy, until we reached the foot of the knoll. As the road angled upward, thorny mimosa bushes clawed the sides of the car and sharp rocks pounded the bottom, as though the hill were trying to repel this wheeled intruder. The sun hung low in the sky when we finally abandoned the car and began hiking up the rutted path.

Approaching the top, we could see the remains of a broken windmill silhouetted against the darkening sky, and hear the chatter of hundreds of cave swallows spiraling above the flattened summit. By the time we reached the hilltop, the circling swallows had formed a vortex. Then, as though some invisible force were sucking them out of the evening sky, they plummeted downward and disappeared. In a matter of minutes, the entire flock was swallowed by a pair of twenty-foot-wide sinkholes that crowned the narrow crest. Though this spectacle was worth the trip, it was only a prelude to the more extravagant wildlife phenomenon soon to follow.

The throaty rasp of the swallows was slowly replaced by the pipping cry of bats—millions of bats. Two cavernous eyes opened on the hillside into an immense chamber that narrowed and disappeared deep within the earth. Bats poured out of the darkened recess and mixed with the swallows still swooping and circling in the cavern. Soon the birds reposed to their mud-cup nests stuck to the domed ceiling, and the bats began to stream forth from the secluded depths of the inner cave. And spewing from the cave with them, fanned by millions of wingbeats, the fetid air of the befouled chambers assaulted our noses and burned our eyes.

Just as the birds had poured into the sinkhole openings in the cranium of the cave, the bats poured out of the two ocular side entrances. An estimated ten million Mexican free-tailed bats inhabit the Frio Bat Cave. As the sunset red deepened to twilight purple, the river of bats reached flood tide, cresting upward and outward, flowing into the darkened sky like a river into the sea. The twisting, surging stream spread out across the horizon until it formed a living alluvial fan against an ocean of whitecap clouds.

Overhead, another spectator had come to view this incredible phenomenon, but with reasons more primal than curiosity. A red-tailed hawk circled above the surging tide of flying mammals. He targeted a single bat, carefully gauged its trajectory, and then made his dive. His fan-shaped tail cupped the air and his three-foot wings momentarily fanned as he swooped over the fluttering river of life. One powerful talon seized a bat like a grizzly plucking a salmon from a rushing mountain brook.

The sky turned black and the stars glistened like lights on a distant ridge, but the bats kept pouring from the cave. Even as we returned to the car and bumped our way slowly through the darkened pasture, the bats continued to vacate their subterranean metropolis. It takes a long time for ten million bats to commute to work, which may be as far as fifty miles from their cave. Air Force radar tracked the bats spiraling from Bracken Cave near San Antonio to an altitude of eleven thousand feet before the flock dispersed, riding the high-altitude winds to distant foraging grounds. A helicopter clocked a flock flying sixty miles per hour.

Among the many bat caves in central Texas, ten shelter between four and twenty million Mexican free-tailed bats, all females, all bearing young. The population doubles with the June birthing. The males live in smaller concentrations in caves, crevices, and under bridges and eves in urban areas. The Congress Avenue bridge over the Colorado River in Austin harbors 250,000 Mexican free-tailed bats, the largest urban concentration of bats in the world. The Texas armada of flying mammals devours approximately 144,000 tons of insects annually.

The sinkholes and caves etched in the Hill Country's limestone mantle provide the perfect home for bats. Rain, ever so slightly acidic from absorbing atmospheric carbon dioxide, slowly eats away at the limestone. After percolating through the rock for countless millennia, the acidified rain has created a labyrinth of dissolution channels and chambers, turning the hills into a massive chunk of Swiss cheese. These underground passages attract more bats and more species of bats than any other place in North America.

In nature's efficient scheme of life, some organisms will adapt to exploit every source of life-giving energy, such as the billions of moths that flutter through the starry night. The moths' nocturnal life-style enable them to avoid diurnal predators, such as the cave swallows that share the bats' cavernous home. But if moths can adapt to the night shift, so can bats. These tiny mammals have developed a sense of sonar unexcelled in the animal kingdom. With faces shaped like miniature dish antennas to focus ultrasonic echoes to their sensitive ears, these sometimes grotesque-looking creatures "see" with a series of high-frequency beeps. Bats are so sensitive to the sonic response that they can detect large background objects, such as trees, at one hundred yards and analyze the size, shape, and texture of closer objects.

The frequency pattern a bat uses depends on the terrain. Mexican free-tailed bats forage high above the open shrub land of the Hill Country, so they are not concerned with dodging trees or other objects. They search for prey using a constant frequency of about ten beeps per second, which indicates the presence of an object but not much else. When pursuing a moth, a bat switches to a faster, frequency-modulated (FM) signal that reveals much more information about the prey. Bats foraging among trees alternate their search signal between constant and modulated beeps.

As I watched the congested stream of bats pouring out of the cave, I couldn't help but compare it to the crowded rush-hour traffic jams of cities. But in contrast to human drivers, these one-third-ounce commuters were able to negotiate the airy freeways without colliding. The only casualties were a few that became entangled in the thorny mesquite trees that bordered the cave. Maybe they just forgot to turn on their FM sonar.

I saw one snagged bat flopping against a thorny limb like a fish on a hook. I carefully clipped away the thorn from its delicate wing membrane with the scissors on my Swiss Army knife. It stared up at me with tiny eyes and uncomprehending brain as I freed it to rejoin its comrades. My own brain was having trouble comprehending the significance of this congregation of ten million creatures, each with a detection system more compact and complex than that produced by the most advanced human technology. We create complex circuitry by arranging molecules of varying conductivity on microscopic crystalline structures, but we cannot come close to duplicating the function of the brain of the tiniest mammal. Nature developed all this sophistication just to enable these creatures to catch moths.

This wildlife spectacle was just too much majesty to comprehend. Staring at the immensity of a starry sky is humbling enough, but then fill that night with ten million furry, flapping creatures, descendants from the same line that produced the upright bipeds we so proudly call *Homo sapiens*. My psyche was overloaded. What is the role of human life on this planet, anyway? How should we of inquisitive mind, but limited knowledge, interact with a system that can produce a bat? We congratulate ourselves on our ability to rocket our species into space or to target deadly missiles on distant cities, but nature surpasses our technology with this diminutive, self-replicating bug catcher. I left that scene with a new sense of awe for the inherent wisdom of the creative force that produced the world and placed me in it.

WILDLIFE DOWN UNDER

Though the caves of the Hill Country host the greatest concentration of mammal life in the world, the minute invertebrates are what excite many scientists. Nourished by a constant supply of spring water and nutrients percolating through the soil, the caves harbor scores of species of spiders, beetles, daddy longlegs, and pseudoscorpions. In addition to these eyeless, colorless arthropods, rare mollusks, fish, and salamanders inhabit the deep recesses of the cave systems. Surrounded by arid countryside, these protected subterranean environments are biological islands as isolated from each other as oases in the Sahara. The isolation has been so complete and so long that many distinct species have evolved that exist in only one or two caves. As many as thirty new invertebrates, as yet unclassified, two snails, and a salamander species have been discovered in caves in the Austin area alone. Who knows what mysteries await discovery in the hundreds of springs and caves hidden throughout the Hill Country?

THE DEER CAPITAL OF THE PLANET EARTH

Bats are not the only mammals in the Hill Country that number in the millions. With 1.5 million white-tailed deer, half the Texas population, the Edwards Plateau ranks as the deer capital of the world. You definitely do not have to strain to see deer in the Hill Country. On any evening dozens wander through the campgrounds in most of the state parks in the area. When you encounter them on a hiking trail, they stare, snort their displeasure, and move a short distance away into deeper cover. A twilight or morning drive, particularly along the less-used back roads, stirs up scores of deer. Frightened by vehicles, herds of five to twenty may dash across the road or vault gracefully over fences. Deer are so numerous feeding along the roadsides that they cause a considerable number of automobile accidents.

Deer hunting is a multimillion-dollar industry in Texas and an important source of income to many ranchers who sell hunting leases to their land. The opening day of deer season in November is as big an event as Thanksgiving. About 175,000 hunters take to the hills in central Texas to test their skills. Yet, despite this army of dedicated hunters, Texas has too many deer for the available resources.

Humans have eradicated the natural predators of the deer, the wolves and cougars. The predators kept the population in balance with the food available by removing the weak, the sick, and the surplus young. This natural selection kept the breeding stock strong, healthy, and stable. In contrast, today's hunters remove the strongest, healthiest males from the breeding pool, leaving the weak and infirm and surplus to compete for the dwindling supplies of food.

White-tailed deer so overpopulate the overgrazed and degraded range of the Hill Country that not enough protein is available to sustain a healthy population at the current numbers. Deer eat little grass, the staple of cattle, but compete directly with sheep, goats, and the growing numbers of exotic animals for herbaceous plants, leaves, acorns, and mesquite pods. Deer need a daily diet of 16 percent protein, which is lacking over most of the Hill Country. Supplemental feeding doesn't solve the problem. Feed corn, commonly sold at service stations during hunting season, contains only 8 percent protein. As a result, Hill Country deer, though the most numerous, are the most malnourished and underdeveloped in the state.

The Edwards Plateau averages one deer per thirteen acres and three and one-half does for every buck. Since 90 percent of the does breed every year, producing one to two fawns each, killing bucks has no appreciable effect on controlling the deer population. If every hunter killed only does every year, the herd would come close to the carrying capacity of the range. But less than 20 percent of the hunters use the antlerless deer permit that comes with every license. Hunters are more interested in bagging trophies than in maintaining a healthy deer herd.

The white-tailed deer captures the imagination of modern humans perhaps more than any other animal. After bluebonnets, deer are probably the most popular subjects for painters and photographers in the Hill Country. Deer are both the symbol of our free spirit and a metaphor of the human relationship with nature. In the Hill Country, the white-tailed deer is tragically out of balance with the environment and plagued by the excesses of an immoderate civilization. Living in a habitat impoverished by human exploitation, they have no hope of reaching their full potential. In this respect, the plight of the white-tailed deer and that of residents living in our impoverished inner cities have great similarities.

On a recent two-day trip on Llano County back roads, I saw roughly one hundred white-tailed deer (a conservative estimate). Each time, they bounded off, running low and fast, then sprang effortlessly over fence and bush. My heart bounded with them. Deer may be gentled by human kindness, but they have never been domesticated. Maybe that is why they captivate us so. In an era when human progress has subjugated so much of nature, the deer remains wild. And the part of us that wishes to escape the snares of our society, that feels hobbled by a life-style that constrains our spirit, yearns to dash away with the fleetness of a white-tailed deer.

WHITE-TAILED DEER (*ODOCOILEUS VIRGINIANUS*)
IN KERRVILLE STATE RECREATION AREA

AN ARMADILLO (*DASYPUS NOVEMCINCTUS*) IN
LOST MAPLES STATE NATURAL AREA

EVENING FLIGHT OF MEXICAN FREETAIL BATS (*TADARIDA BRASILIENSIS*) AROUND THEIR CAVE NEAR THE FRIO RIVER

LOST MAPLES STATE NATURAL AREA

CAN CREEK IN LOST MAPLES STATE NATURAL AREA

THRILLS IN THE TREETOPS

*"If future generations are to remember us more with
gratitude than with sorrow, we must achieve more than
the miracles of technology. We must also leave them a
glimpse of the world as it was created, not just as it
looked when we got through with it."*
*Lyndon B. Johnson, from a letter sent by the Texas Nature
Conservancy to its members, May 9, 1988*

Excitement comes in small packages in the Hill Country. In March and April, the central-Texas sun begins spreading that resinous, baked cedar smell across the hills. Then spring thunderstorms add a freshness that makes you feel like you are breathing in the renewal of life itself. At such times a distinct breed of humans descends on the oak-juniper canyons and the oak thicketed slopes of the Hill Country: the bird watchers. They come with binoculars, field guides, checklists, and high gain tape recorders, seeking a glimpse of two rare birds. Each spring, the golden-cheeked warbler and the black-capped vireo wing their way to Texas from their wintering grounds in Central America. Both are endangered with extinction because of the widespread destruction of their nesting habitat in the Hill Country.

Every golden-cheeked warbler in existence is a native Texan. Though they spend their winters in Guatemala, Nicaragua, and Honduras, these four-inch birds have chosen the Hill Country exclusively to rear their children. By mid-March, they have made their perilous migration and are busily setting up housekeeping. They nest only on slopes and canyons where the magic combination of live oaks, Texas oaks, and Ashe junipers occurs. The woodlands must be mature, about fifty years old, to attract the warbler. The colorful little birds adhere rigidly to an ancient building code and weave their nests of juniper bark bound with spider webs. They fatten their young on the caterpillars that infest the oak trees.

Golden-cheeks live in about forty counties in central Texas. Their prime nesting habitat stretches from the Colorado River north of Austin south to San Antonio and west toward Edwards County. Their crescent-shaped territory, about fifty miles wide and one hundred fifty miles long, corresponds to the rapidly disappearing cedar brakes of the Hill Country. As impounded rivers flood wooded canyons, urban sprawl dices prime nesting areas, and ranching activities eradicate the junipers, more and more of the birds' habitat disappears or becomes substandard.

Because of its specialized nesting preference, this warbler disappears when the juniper is eliminated. Early in 1990, the United States Fish and Wildlife Agency placed the golden-cheeked warbler on the list of animals threatened with extinction. In March 1990, golden-cheeks were given an emergency endangered listing because of increasing loss of habitat in urban areas. The listing protected the birds for 240 days while a permanent listing was considered. On December 27, 1990, the permanent listing was granted.

You can hear the buzzing *biz-bizz-bizz-biz* of a golden-cheeked warbler singing from an exposed limb or treetop, but you must search the brushy thickets for the elusive black-capped vireo. Unlike the forest-dwelling warbler, this endangered vireo inhabits waist-high thickets of scrubby shin oak. Black-caps breed in scattered locations from northern Mexico through central Texas into Oklahoma. Along the eastern boundary of the Hill Country, which receives thirty to thirty-five inches of rainfall annually, the oak shinneries they favor have a limited lifetime. Within twenty years or so, the thicket matures into a woodland.

In times before settlers tamed the hills, wildfires periodically swept across the rocky terrain. Grasses covered the cleared areas, then dense brush and shin oak thickets invaded the grassy openings. The black-capped vireo nests in this mid-successional habitat, perhaps because few other birds share that particular niche. And it is a particular niche. In the Hill Country, this distinctive vegetational combination occurs primarily on outcroppings of the Fredericksburg limestone group. The thinner soils cannot support oaks, and the richer clays sustain the oak-juniper woodlands favored by the golden-cheeked warbler. In the more drought-stressed western section of the Edwards Plateau, the oak shinneries are the climax vegetation and provide a more permanent home for this discriminating vireo.

Like the golden-cheeked warbler, the vireo suffers from loss of habitat. The same economic forces that condemn cedar brakes eradicate oak shinneries. In addition, the vireo has to contend with another result of human influence that may eventually drive it to extinction: the brown-headed cowbird. Besides destroying vireo habitat, ranching and land-clearing activities encourage a growing population of cowbirds.

Cowbirds, members of the blackbird clan, glean the grain scattered wherever livestock are fed. The spillage sustains large flocks of English sparrows, blackbirds, and other opportunistic feeders. With ample food, compliments of humans, all the brown-headed cowbird needs to flourish is a place to lay its eggs, which it preempts from vireos and warblers. The cowbird seeks out an active nest, removes an egg, and lays its own. Unable to discern the interloper's eggs or hatchlings, the foster parents rear the parasite bird. The cowbird nestling kills the other young, and when mature, joins its kin.

Every cowbird in the massive flocks that congregate around farm and ranch lots represents a sacrificed clutch of eggs for some other species. The average songbird nest produces about three fledglings, so one hundred cowbirds translates into three hundred fewer vireos and warblers. Sometimes the host birds can rear a second clutch of eggs, so the breeding season is not completely lost, but second clutches are seldom as successful as the first. As black-capped vireo numbers drop due to loss of habitat, the assault of cowbirds threatens to swamp them into extinction. In some areas, cowbirds parasitize almost every vireo nest. Federal recovery programs for the endangered vireo include cowbird trapping and removal from the vireo's nesting areas.

One of the features that makes the Hill Country so attractive to insectivorous birds like vireos and warblers is the abundant population of insects. Though pasture improvement and cedar eradication alter the environment, much of the Hill Country contains a relatively undisturbed and intact ecosystem. One scientist estimated that twenty-five million insects live from the ground up in each square mile of undisturbed environment.

Each spring, just as the live oaks are getting their new leaves, caterpillars appear by the millions. In bad years (for the trees), the voracious little eating machines completely denude every live oak for miles and miles. When the wind blows, tiny little pellets of caterpillar excrement shower down with a rainlike pitter-patter on the dry leaves. But even in their wholesale assault on the trees, the caterpillars have a majestic effect.

When the afternoon sun drops low in the sky, creating long shadows and warm reflections, each infested live oak takes on a fairyland appearance. Thousands of glistening threads hang from the limbs. The streamers ripple in the evening breeze, flashing silver and gold in the fading light. A closer inspection of this phenomenon reveals that each thread supports a squirming worm. The vision pops into my mind of a group of aberrant fishermen snagging their baited lines on the overhanging limbs and leaving in frustration.

When the caterpillars are not feasting on oak leaves, they escape the hungry warblers, vireos, and other insectivorous birds by dangling in midair. Like tiny marionettes suspended on gossamer threads, they sway back and forth in the breeze, dancing to the tune of survival. Despite the assault of the worms, the trees survive and produce another crop of leaves after the caterpillars abandon their earthbound existence. Emerging as moths, they soar into the sky to be greeted by a host of hungry flycatchers, swallows, and bats. More than one hundred species of birds breed in the Hill Country, satisfying the voracious appetites of their young with the abundant supply of creeping, crawling, and flying insects.

A QUESTION OF VALUE

Should developers stop building houses, and should ranchers stop improving their pastures so minuscule warblers and vireos can have a place to raise their young? What good is a warbler, anyway? Such questions come from our consumer-oriented, egocentric value system. Must we value an animal or plant only for the financial gain or physical pleasure we derive from it? This exploitative attitude indicates that we have lost the wonder, awe, and respect for the life force that sustains this fragile planet we call home.

Pictures of birds in field guides, whether painted or photographed, cannot capture the vivacious character of a bird—that animation that mesmerizes every bird watcher. I remember my first April in the steamy cedar brake trailing the elusive trill of a golden-cheek. Suddenly, a brightly colored male popped out of the brush onto a branch a few feet above me, threw back his head, and unabashedly sang his song. I could see his blazing yellow cheeks and jet-black eye stripe, cap, and collar. My heart stopped. Life exuded from this tiny bird with fiery eye and buzzing song. I felt a rush of exhilaration. For a second, as he poured his soul into the air, I felt a oneness with this fellow traveler, a union that transcended the superior attitude characteristic of our species. So what that this feathered creature could not divine the mysteries of the physical universe and build great machines that dive the ocean depths and soar beyond the skies? It possessed the basic characteristic that propels all life from birth to grave: the will to live out its life from day to day with zeal and determination. That quality alone should be a unifying force that binds us to all other life forms sharing this planet.

A GOLDEN-CHEEKED WARBLER (*DENDROICA CHRYSOPARIA*)
IN HAYS COUNTY

A MOCKINGBIRD (*MIMUS POLYGLOTTOS*)

A CACTUS WREN (*CAMPYLORHYNCHUS BRUNNEICAPILLUS*)

A PIED-BILLED GREBE (*PODILYMBUS PODICEPS*)

CLIFF SWALLOWS (*HIRUNDO PYRRHONOTA*) ON
THE FRIO RIVER IN REAL COUNTY

WHITE PRICKLY POPPY (*ARGEMONE ALBIFLORA*)
IN LLANO COUNTY

WILDFLOWERS AND RARE PLANTS

*"Flowers have changed the face of the planet. Without
them, the world we know—even man himself—
would never have existed."*
Loren Eiseley, The Immense Journey

When Texans thinks of hillsides blanketed with wildflowers, they think of the Hill Country. Calendar scenes of fields decorated with bluebonnets and Indian paintbrushes adorn our walls and are the favorite subjects for painters throughout the state. Add a windmill or a weathered barn and you have an artist's or photographer's delight. Nature photographers from around the nation journey to central Texas to capture the beauty of the more than 425 species of flowering plants that greet the spring. The state highway department cooperates by seeding the roadsides and delaying mowing in the spring until the flowers have cast their seeds for next year's crop.

It's a classic understatement to say that Texans love and are proud of their wildflowers. Lady Bird Johnson epitomized that pride when she established the National Wildflower Research Center in Austin. *Texas Highways* magazine dedicates its April issue to wildflowers, and each year more new books appear that glorify nature's colorful display. Year after year, the best-selling books in the state are the wildflower field guides.

But the gorgeous displays of wildflowers are not the only plants that make the Hill Country botanically special. The secluded canyons and spring-fed streams nestled in the remote hills harbor rare plants found nowhere else in the world. In addition to these endemics, seven species of plants occur that grow in fewer than six localities globally, and some fifteen more occur in fewer than twenty localities.

As the most recent Ice Age began to wane some ten thousand years ago, Texas became progressively hotter and drier. Plants better suited to arid conditions slowly replaced the forests that once covered much of west Texas. Today, only a few isolated populations of those relics of a moister epoch remain. Some, such as the bigtooth maple, maintain a toehold in the protected microclimates of steep-walled, spring-fed canyons in central and west Texas. With the right autumn temperature and moisture conditions, this small-leaved maple paints canyon slopes with brilliant hues of red, yellow, and burgundy. These maples line the canyons of the Sabinal River and its twisting tributaries near Vanderpool. Toward the end of October, thousands of people make the annual pilgrimage to Lost Maples State Natural Area to witness a colorful pageant rare for Texas trees.

Other plants have evolved with the changing climate and now thrive in an environment much more arid than that of their closest relatives. Unlike other pinyon pines that grow at 4,500- to 6,500-foot elevations in the Southwest, the remote pinyon, *Pinus remota*, is right at home on the arid limestone hills east of the Pecos River. Once while tromping across the rocky hills in Edwards County, I came upon a stand of the rare pines. They seemed so out of place, but not as out of place as the porcupine hiding in the top of one of them. (These waddling, barbed creatures are fairly common throughout the Hill Country and west Texas.) Under the pines was another rare plant, rare in the wild, that is: the red yucca, *Hesperaloe parvifolia*. Though not a yucca, this related member of the agave family has a tall blooming stalk decorated with red flowers. This attractive, drought-tolerant plant is popular in landscapes from Texas to California.

Another rare tree, the Texas madrone, sometimes called naked lady's leg because of its slick pink bark, grows in mountain canyons of the Trans-Pecos. But a small population survives on the dry, rocky hillsides along the crescent southern boundary of the Hill Country from Austin to Leakey. These evergreen members of the blueberry family are also finding their way into home and commercial landscapes as Texans become more conscious of the beauty and maintenance-free qualities of native plants.

East meets west in the Hill Country, with plants of eastern distribution rubbing shoulders with more western species. The sandy soil of the Llano Uplift supports eastern trees such as hickory and post oak. At Lost Maples, witch hazel, common in the east Texas piney woods, grows besides the western bigtooth maple. A disjunct population of red bay, an aromatic tree of the sandy piney woods and coastal plains, grows on the limestone creek banks below Hamilton Pool, a popular swimming hole west of Austin. The list goes on with Torrey yucca from the desert cohabitating with Carolina basswood from the east, with palmetto palms from the coast finding a home in spring-fed creeks, and with wildflowers from both sides of the state making seasonal invasions into alien territory.

The Hill Country is home for some species normally associated with the tropics. A cedar brake makes an unlikely place for an orchid, but that's where I had been instructed to look for the crested coralroot. As I dodged under the spreading juniper limbs, the burrlike needles collected under my shirt collar and crept down my back like angry ants. The brake concealed the charred, weathered stumps left by cedar choppers half a century earlier, burrows of armadillos dug under boulder outcroppings for want of deeper soil, and somewhere the six-inch stem of a dainty orchid. Finally, I found the flower and set up my flash to document this unusual plant with the imposing name of *Hexalectris spicata*.

Another orchid, the giant hellebore, *Epipactis gigantea*, finds a foothold in moist, rocky soil along seeps and creeks. The blooms decorating the eighteen-inch stalk of this "giant" are barely one-fourth of an inch wide. If one orchid is a surprise, two orchids aren't enough for these rocky, arid hills. A third, the jasmine-scented *Spiranthes cernua*, or ladies' tresses orchid, pokes its eight- to twelve-inch stem through the caliche and grass. Like miniature maypole decorations, scores of tiny white flowers twist around the petite stem. The aroma attracts black-and-yellow-striped bumble bees that cling to the tiny stalks as they dance in the breeze.

These terrestrial orchids conceal one of the most mysterious relationships found in nature. It's a strange marriage, but these elegant plants cannot survive without the help of a soil fungus. The fungi find shelter in the outer portion of the roots and, in turn, produce nutrients that the roots absorb. This unusual bed-and-breakfast arrangement makes transplanting terrestrial orchids or growing them from seeds almost impossible. Some forty-seven species of orchids grow in Texas, most in the moist soil of east Texas.

The list of Hill Country rarities grows as botanists explore the sheltered canyons and rugged slopes. Small populations of Texas snowbell, *Styrax texana*, and canyon mock orange, *Philadelphus ernestii*, cling to existence on sheer canyon walls out of reach of hungry deer and goats. A small population of a red sage, *Salvia penstemoniodes*, long thought extinct, was recently rediscovered. Now the plant, with its striking red, penstemonlike blooms and three-foot stalk, is growing in gardens across the state as native-plant enthusiasts spread its seeds.

In this day of advanced technology and bustling cities, the Hill Country still harbors undiscovered treasures. Its remoteness, ruggedness, and rigorous climate have created unique biological niches where rare life forms thrive. And like a protective parent, these qualities have safeguarded its rare plants and animals from the encroachment of creeping subdivisions, the marauding plow of agriculture, and the noxious effluent of industry.

BLUEBONNETS (*LUPINUS TEXENSIS*)
AND BLADDERPODS
(*LESQUERELLA* SPECIES) IN LLANO COUNTY

MULLEIN (*VERBASCUM THAPSUS*) LEAVES

MEXICAN BUCKEYE FLOWERS
(*UNGNADIA SPECIOSA*)

CLARET CUP CACTI
(*ECHINOCEREUS TRIGLOCHIDIATUS*)
IN LLANO COUNTY

THE WHITE ELEPHANT SALOON, BUILT IN 1888.
THE WHITE ELEPHANT IS THOUGHT TO HAVE BEEN AN OLD GERMAN
SYMBOL FOR A DRINKING AND EATING ESTABLISHMENT.

INDIAN, GERMANS, AND COWBOYS

"There ain't no doubt at all," continued Uncle Seth,
"that the Spaniards, who were terrible fellers
for nosing out gold and silver, did work a
good many mines in this region, and some day when the
country settles up they will be found."
J. C. Duval, Early Times in Texas

Once, before such activities were prohibited, I took my bedroll and spent the night on top of Enchanted Rock. I nested in a rocky depression surrounded by stunted live oaks and prickly pears. The night was moonless, lit only by the distant lanterns of the stars. In such blackness, broken only by the restless fingers of the wind and the repetitive chirp of crickets, time takes on a different dimension.

Time is a tenuous artifact supported by the props that surround our daily lives. Remove the rumble of distant thoroughfares, the omnipresent light of the city, and the constant intrusion of television. Then time loses its rigidity and begins to dance in step with imagination's tune. That night on the windy crest of the weather-worn granite dome, history came to life for me as it never had in a classroom. The year was placed not by the calendar hanging in my office, but by my mind. Once again on that summer night, this was Comanche country.

As I lay under the stars in a Twilight Zone state of mind, I could almost hear a war party of Comanche creeping up the granite slopes. At any moment the marauding Indians would come whooping over the crest, just as they had in 1841. If Texas Ranger John Hays could drive them off this lonely rock with his rifle, I hoped I could master these phantoms with the powers of my mind. But as I stared at the multitude of stars, the same stars that blinked while Captain Hays slid away in the dark to rejoin his compatriots, I could still hear the feisty snort of mustangs in the distance and the groaning of ox-drawn wagons bringing those early settlers into a hostile land.

In 1840, a group of German nobles formed the Society for the Protection of German Immigrants, called the Adelsverein, and presented Texas as the land of promise. It may have been the first real estate debacle in Texas, but it changed the history of the state. The Adelsverein had acquired a three-million-acre grant between the Llano and Colorado rivers, and promised settlers 640 acres of rich farmland. Some seven thousand Germans answered the call of adventure and fortune before the Adelsverein folded in about 1845. The German settlers arrived in the port of Indianola and made their way to New Braunfels, the first town established for the newcomers. In 1846, John Meusebach, commissioner general of the Adelsverein, pushed eighty miles farther west toward their goal and founded Fredericksburg. Staking claim to their new homeland proved harder than they had expected.

During World Wars I and II, patriots bragged that the United States had never been invaded by a hostile enemy. The Native Americans would disagree (as would the heroes of the Alamo). In the 1840s, the Apache and Comanche were the landlords of the Hill Country. Their might and determination had repelled the powerful Spanish conquistadors a century before. Now the Germans and Anglo-Saxons had the temerity to come with their families and set up housekeeping. In a bloodthirsty conflict where terror was their most powerful weapon, the Indians swooped through the sparsely populated territory. They killed, raped, kidnapped, and burned all in their path. Posses of settlers, Texas Rangers, and army troops relentlessly pursued the raiding parties, and often returned with stolen horses and braided scalps decorating their belts.

Enchanted Rock derives its name from the meaning of the word *enchanted* that implies "bewitched." The superstitious believed that spirits possessed the dome, which protrudes 445 feet above the surrounding countryside. Mirrorlike reflections from puddles of water on its top and weird creaking sounds from thermal expansion of the rock convinced Indians and settlers alike that this was a home of the spirits. That night I spent alone on the rock convinced me that this barren expanse of granite is indeed a place of power. The saga of Indian warriors and tenacious settlers still lives in the dark nights of the hills.

The fearless Apache chief Big Foot stalked these cedar-covered hills and even invaded Austin to steal horses. Equally fearless frontiersmen, such as Big Foot Wallace, named after the Indian chief, defended their newly acquired land. Outnumbered and outgunned, the Indians had no chance of lasting victory. In 1873 a group of eight Texans trailed twenty-three marauding Indians. They attacked them in the dead of night on Packsaddle Mountain near Llano. The last Indian raid along the Sabinal River occurrred in 1876 when Comanche killed sixteen people and escaped with a large herd of stolen horses into Mexico. April, 1881 saw the last Indian raid in the Hill Country. A party of Lipan Apache killed a family north of Leakey and fled into Mexico. The 25th Infantry of Seminoles from Fort Clark pursued them across the Rio Grande. The soldiers surrounded their mountain encampment during the night and attacked at dawn.

The most famous Indian legend of the area, however, is not of hostility, but of promised peace. When John Meusebach established Fredericksburg in 1846 with one hundred and twenty adults and children, the area was in the heart of Indian territory. Those European farmers suddenly found themselves fighting for their lives with the fiercest warriors of the plains, the Comanche. The Indians were fighting for survival and they made the rules: terror, torture, and no prisoners. After a year of Indian hostilities, Meusebach arranged a meeting with the Comanche near the present town of Menard. As Meusebach's party left Fredericksburg, Indian scouts built fires in the hills to signal that no troops followed. Parents told frightened children that the fires were not hostile Indians but bunnies boiling wildflowers to color Easter eggs. Meusebach secured the land between the Llano and San Saba rivers and a pledge of peace from the Comanche for $1,000 in goods. Lighting fires in the hills to celebrate the treaty developed into the Easter Fires Pageant, a tradition still celebrated in Fredericksburg.

By the end of the 1870s, the Indians had been driven out of the Hill Country, and settlers flooded across the limestone hills like a swollen river. The next twenty years saw the birth, boom, and bust of the great cattle drives and the establishment of the German culture as the dominant influence. In those times of rapid change, the alchemy of the steep-walled canyons and spring-fed streams worked its magic on the people, the culture, and the economy.

The mute hills that for centuries had echoed the hoof beats of Indian ponies now reverberated with accents from central Europe. The Adelsverein colonists brought the Teutonic culture into the very heart of Texas. Their wedge-shaped holdings bisected the Edwards Plateau from New Braunfels at the southeastern border to Mason on the northwestern edge. They settled Comal, Kendal, Gillespie, and Mason counties.

A dark, starry night and the moaning wind on top of Enchanted Rock isolated me from the reality of my world. I felt acutely alone and disjointed. But that was nothing compared to the culture shock of those early Germans. Farmers accustomed to following an ox-drawn plow down parallel furrows found themselves herding cattle and goats in an Hispanic-based economy. But their livelihood was not all that the alchemy of the hills transmuted. Early Methodist evangelists in Fredericksburg attracted a large and faithful following of immigrants. When the opportunity arose in the 1850s, the teetotaling Wesleyan Germans moved en masse to the Llano River valley in Mason County. These Texas Germans no longer lifted their steins to toast a successful harvest; they hoisted their canteens of water and saddled up for a day on the range.

The magic of the Hill Country not only turned German farmers into Texas cowboys, but also transformed sane and stable people into dream chasers. Treasure hunters, invariably optimistic and usually gullible, scoured the hills searching for the Lost Bowie Mine, the Lost San Saba Mine, the Lizard Mine (with gold nuggets as large as lizards), and cedar brake caches of Spanish bullion. The Spanish started the fever in 1757 when they established the presidio of San Luis de las Amarillas on the north bank of the San Saba to mine a rich silver lode. Comanche ravaged the fort, leaving only legends of the mine to haunt future generations.

Legend attests that only the Indians knew the location of the rich veins of silver and gold, and they guarded their secret well. Only Jim Bowie gained their trust, and his newly acquired knowledge perished with him at the Alamo. As decades turned into centuries, the legends grew to include not only concealed mother lodes, but also treasures of bullion buried by the conquistadors. In their haste to escape marauding Indians, the Spanish reportedly buried fortunes of gold and silver.

Many a prospector ordered another round and listened carefully to tales of accidental discovery. Cowboys reported discoveries of old smelters and nearby sinkholes or caves piled high with bars of silver or gold. Other treasure seekers had authentic maps to guide them to an obscure circle on Packsaddle Mountain that pointed to the mouth of a hidden mine shaft. Or someone told of a map briefly seen and half remembered that cryptically described the location of a mine or buried treasure. Those who accidently discovered the rich lodes invariably met with untimely deaths, or unavoidable circumstances prevented their return. Naturally, they told their secret of untold wealth with their last breaths.

Several facts stand clear from all the stories of lost mines and concealed treasure: Early settlers were extremely busy and seldom had time to scoop up the fortunes they found; they could track a war party for a hundred miles but invariably became disoriented when trying to return to a mine; and bad luck invariably hounded those whose eyes had gazed on fortune. The locations of untold treasures in the Hill Country remain untold, hidden somewhere on Packsaddle Mountain, along the shores of the San Saba River, or Honey Creek, or Los Moros Creek, or in some steep-walled canyon on the headwaters of the Frio.

The night I spent atop Enchanted Rock was long, interrupted by the back and forth flow of history. The approach of dawn gradually transformed the black sky into gray, then pushed it through the transient hint of gold into the cold reality of blue. The phantom-chasing light dispelled my dreams of marauding Comanche, desperate settlers, and deluded treasure seekers. Standing alone, facing the wind and the warming rays of first light, I felt my mind slip back into the secure glove of modern reality, but since then the fit has never been quite as tight. The Hill Country can do that, you know.

CATTLE IN GILLESPIE COUNTY

A PEACH (*PRUNUS PERSICA*) TREE

A PEACH (*PRUNUS PERSICA*) BLOSSOM

PHLOX AND A TEXAS STAR (*LINDHEIMERA TEXANA*)
IN BURNET COUNTY

ENCHANTED ROCK STATE NATURAL AREA

A CLARET CUP (*ECHINOCEREUS TRIGLOCHIDIATUS*)
AND BLUEBONNETS (*LUPINUS TEXENSIS*)
IN GILLESPIE COUNTY

RESTORED LOG HOUSE AT LYNDON B. JOHNSON'S
NATIONAL HISTORIC PARK, JOHNSON CITY

LEGACY OF A FRONTIERSMAN

"All my life I have drawn sustenance from the rivers
and hills of my native state. . . . I want no
less for all the children of America than
what I was privileged to have as a boy."
Lyndon B. Johnson, from an inscription in the museum at
the Lyndon B. Johnson National Historic Park

The land: You just can't separate the land from the man. To touch the heart of the Hill Country is to touch the heart of the thirty-sixth president of the United States, Lyndon Baines Johnson. Psychiatrists say we're influenced by two factors as we grow up: nature (our genetic inheritance), and nurture (our home life and surroundings). Johnson grew up in a land and time that sculpted its impressionable youth with the rasp of hardship. For those who endured, it honed a cutting edge on their will to succeed. If the land had been more gentle, Johnson might have slipped out of its grip. But he never forgot his roots. He never became softened and smoothed by the influence of big city, big government, big money.

Lyndon Johnson was a frontiersman. He was probably the last president ever to be born at home and delivered by a midwife. His grandfather fought in the Civil War and had gotten rich and gone bust driving cattle north on the Chisholm Trail. His father raised cotton, but was more politician than farmer, and often took his oldest son to Austin to sit at his side in the Legislature. Lyndon grew up with politics the way most kids grow up with baseball cards. He learned at an early age that it took some shrewd dealing to get the best cards.

The Hill Country ethic is simple: Work hard and just maybe you won't starve. As a youth, Lyndon ran trap lines and shined shoes. After high school, he washed dishes and picked fruit in California. Back in Johnson City, he drove a truck and worked on a road crew building the highway in front of what would one day be the Texas White House. Apparently, somewhere during this personal vision quest, Lyndon decided his father had the right idea. Politics was better than sweat as a vehicle for success.

Lyndon enrolled in college in San Marcos, just fifty miles from his place of birth. He earned a teacher's certificate and taught public school, but never took his eyes off politics. In 1931, one year after graduating, he made his way to Washington as secretary to a congressman. Six years later, as a freshman congressman, he would be hiring his own secretary.

When Johnson was elected to Congress in 1937, the Hill Country was one of the poorest, most backward areas in the nation. The Depression had assaulted its ranchers and farmers like a Comanche war party. Bankers foreclosed, eastern merchants refused credit, and the unforgiving weather punished the struggling survivors. Had anything really changed in this rugged, isolated country in the last one hundred years? Farmers still harnessed their mules and wrestled their plows as the blade careened through the rocky earth. Ranchers still spent their days in the saddle and hoped hard winters and hungry coyotes wouldn't take too many lambs. Wives still hauled water from their shallow wells, hoed their gardens, canned and baked, and buried too many of their children. Folks trimmed their coal oil lamps at night, socialized at the general store on Saturday, and rode to church in their wagons on Sunday. No telephone lines connected the tiny communities scattered through the rolling hills. No cars, electricity, supermarkets, or movies. At least they didn't have to fight Indians.

Much has been written about Lyndon Johnson and his politics, his humble upbringing, and his quest for power and riches. One things is clear about his life: The Hill Country imprinted him with the horror of destitution. He was determined to rise above the hopeless hardship of poverty and to bring his "fellow Amer'cans" up with him. In his first four years in Congress, he brought electricity to the Hill Country. His fellow congressmen soon learned to court, not contest, this rowdy Texan who carried the genes of a grandfather who had fought Indians and trailed longhorns.

With his conquer-or-be-conquered approach to life, Lyndon waged war on poor education, poverty, racism, and inadequate health care. As president, his landmark legislation brought the nation out of the Depression mentality into the Space Age. And he never forgot his roots. He signed legislation that reorganized the postal department on the steps of the feed store/post office in Hye, Texas, where he had mailed his first letter at age four. He signed into law the landmark higher education bill in his first school house on the banks of the Pedernales River, within walking distance of his birthplace. Johnson believed that an education was the best passport out of poverty. Between Lincoln and Kennedy, Congress enacted only six education bills. During his tenure, Johnson pushed through sixty education bills.

Johnson's vision and endurance took him from a backward town on the banks of a temperamental river to the mansion on the Potomac. He went from freshman congressman just out of college to the Chief of State in only thirty-two years. But the Hill Country fight-all-odds-to-survive way of life finally sealed his political fate. He tried to deal with Vietnam just as his ancestors had dealt with Indians, flash floods, and a failing economy. He carried the power of the presidency to its maximum and was forced to retreat. Vietnam represented not just a military defeat: it indicated that the country was imposing a limit on the authority and power of the executive branch.

Paradoxically, the overt use of military force in Vietnam eventually undermined the might-makes-right mentality that had dominated American thought since the Revolution. To many, it clarified the difference between patriotism, pride in our country, and unbridled nationalism, the belief that, as Stephen Decatur said a century earlier, "our country, may she always be right, but our country right or wrong." The debacle paved the way for tolerance of other political philosophies, a prerequisite for the peace that Lyndon Johnson struggled so hard to achieve.

Lyndon Johnson is buried on the banks of his beloved Pedernales River (pronounced "pur-dah-nal-es"), which flows through his ranch. But his legacy lives on. It lives on because it is not his alone, it belongs to all folks bred of the Hill Country. Lyndon Johnson mirrored the qualities of a land hard with rocky hills yet soft with fern-lined springs, of rivers that would rampage one week and trickle the next, of a land that would slap you as hard as a lightning bolt, then court you with a gown of delicate wildflowers. The heart of Texas tempers its children. One became president. All share its strength.

THE LEGACY LIVES ON

For a celebrity's birthday party, it was a down-home, Texas-style event. A high school band played "Happy Birthday," people came from as far as South Dakota and Georgia, and colorful wildflowers covered the three-tier cake. The party commemorated the fifth anniversary of a dream come true for the First Lady of Wildflowers, Lady Bird Johnson, as well as her seventy-fifth birthday.

Mrs. Johnson arrived wearing a vest embroidered with primroses, paintbrushes, and bluebonnets, and a smile as big as her home state. Today was special. She was savoring a fruit made sweet by years of anticipation. Five years previously, on her seventieth birthday, Mrs. Johnson had given the nation an extraordinary gift: She had established the National Wildflower Research center in Austin. Founding the center revealed a strong but little-known quality in the former First Lady: the ability to wait. She had postponed work on the Wildflower Center for fourteen years, a difficult task for a person known all her life as a doer.

Though in the shadow of her husband, Mrs. Johnson lived the life of an activist for thirty-eight years in Washington, D.C. She helped set up the Head Start Program, founded the First Lady's Committee to Beautify the Capitol, and initiated a program to plant trees in the nation's cities, parks, and roadsides. But wildflowers were her passion, and she saw them disappearing at an alarming rate across the country. She desperately wanted to do something, but other projects had to come first.

"When we left Washington, the first thing was working with the LBJ Library and the LBJ School of Public Affairs at the University of Texas," she said. "Then came the park along the riverfront in my other favorite capital, Austin, and the Highway Beautification Awards." The river cleanup program that she initiated transformed the debris-choked shores of Town Lake in Austin into a showplace river walk lined with a hike and bike trail, blooming trees, gazebos, and gardens. The Texas Highways Beautification Awards Program honors the state highway district with the most attractive landscape planting each year. With these projects completed, Lady Bird at last had time to work on her lifelong ambition: saving a place for wildflowers.

At the Wildflower Center's fifth anniversary party, Mrs. Johnson sat down with a piece of birthday cake and, smiling, said, "When I reached my seventieth birthday, I thought, well now, the crop's in the barn, the children are grown and gone, and now I can do just what I want." But she admits that it was not an easy task.

"Her greatest obstacle was fear that this might not be important enough to do," said Betty Tilson, Mrs. Johnson's personal secretary since 1963.

"I've been crazy about wildflowers all my life, but I always felt apologetic," Lady Bird said. "It may seem like a lightweight proposition in a world of heavyweight problems. And it is, of course. But I love it.

"When I started working on the Wildflower Center, I was scared, I didn't know what to expect. But I decided that regardless of how well or how modestly it succeeds, I'm going to DO it! I pushed and shoved, encouraged and aided, and did everything I could."

Typical of the Johnson legacy, Lady Bird launched the Center with a bang by donating $125,000 and sixty acres on the Colorado River east of Austin. The narrow farm-to-market highway to the Center cuts through fields of sorghum and other crops planted in the rich flood plain soil. The entrance is typical of a Texas ranch: A carved wooden sign hangs over the cattle guard, and a long one-lane drive lined with mesquite trees leads to the headquarters. A small complex of unpretentious buildings sits on a wooded bluff overlooking the river.

Ripples of wind sweep across the acres of coastal Bermuda grass covering the flat expanse surrounding the center. For decades cattle grazed the land that is now the heart of wildflower research in the United States. Square plots marked with red flags and string stretch across prairie like a patchwork quilt. The center itself consists of two greenhouses and an attractive single-story building. Attached to one end is a portable building donated by a bank. Colorful beds of wildflowers line the sidewalk and front porch. The center has an herbarium, a resource library, and dissecting scopes, but the cutting edge of research follows the plow, or flail mower to be exact.

"We study the plants' germination requirements, growth, and flowering periods, and the influence of soil and climate," said Dr. David Northington, Executive Director, "and we conduct natural history and ecological studies. We have ninety wildflower plots, and several large-scale planting areas where we conduct our studies, as well as our greenhouses."

"Wildflowers are hardy survivors," Mrs. Johnson tells the subscribing members of the Research Center, "but the frustrating fact is that little is known about how best to propagate and grow them. Less than two hundred of the twenty-five thousand or so spe-

70

cies have been researched. It's my eager hope that the National Wildflower Research Center will be able to unlock some of their secrets in my lifetime—and 'spread the word' about them."

Since the National Wildflower Research Center began spreading the word, its influence has reached every state in the nation. "Our goal is to promote the conservation and use of wildflowers and other native plants," said Annie Paulson, Resource Botanist. Besides conducting original research, the center develops educational programs and serves as a clearinghouse to disseminate information.

"As a clearinghouse, we often are the first place people turn when they have questions," Paulson said. "We get calls and letters from individuals, botanical gardens, seed companies, universities, highway departments, and other state agencies. Last year we received twenty-six thousand inquiries. Besides wildflowers, we gather data on native trees, shrubs, and grasses, on-site analysis and restoration, and highway department beautification programs. The clearinghouse is forming a nationwide network with a computerized database for easy retrieval and exchange of information.

"So far, we have fact sheets on forty-two states," said Paulson. "When people call, we can send lists of suggested wildflowers and other native plants adapted to their area and where to buy them. We have how-to sheets telling when, where, and how to plant, and a list of resource people in their area. Also, we can supply detailed fact sheets on more than three hundred species of wildflowers."

The effectiveness and usefulness of the clearinghouse was recently demonstrated. "One day I received phone calls from three different state highway departments wanting information on roadside beautification," said Paulson. "Congress passed a law requiring twenty-five cents of every one hundred dollars of federal money granted to states for highway landscaping be used for wildflowers and native plants. We were able to supply the information they needed."

For Mrs. Johnson, saving wildflowers goes far beyond her past beautification projects, which blanketed Washington with so many tulips that a Dutch bulb exporter named a new variety after her. "I wish someone would help me find a better word than beautification," she said. "To some it has a trivial, cosmetic sound. But what it really means is a clean place with order, enhanced with trees and flowers."

"Mrs. Johnson considers beautification a major facet of conservation," said her secretary, Betty Tilson. "It encompasses clean air, clean water, and a variety of issues. It's really an environmental movement. You can't have wildflowers unless you preserve the habitat."

"Beyond the aesthetic value for planting wildflowers," Mrs. Johnson said, "are other valid reasons for their use. As we experience problems with lowering water tables and rising maintenance costs, incorporating nature's bounty into our landscapes may provide a viable alternative to manicured clipped grass."

You don't have to be around Lady Bird long to realize that wildflowers are her passion. "For me," she said, "wildflowers are joy-giving. They enrich my life and feed my soul and give beautiful memories to sustain me. Wildflowers occupy the center stage of my life these days . . . they calm my heart. For my seven grandchildren and everybody else's, I believe we can keep our heritage of wildflowers alive in our public and private landscapes."

Each spring, thousands of people enjoy the wildflowers along Ranch Road 1, which winds alongside the LBJ ranch and through LBJ State Park. Recently, a friend of mine was taking pictures of her children sitting in a spot blanketed with colorful wildflowers. She saw a car slow down and stop a short distance away. The car just sat there, its passenger silently observing the family enjoying the beautiful Hill Country setting. Then the driver pulled contentedly away and turned into the ranch.

No, wildflowers are not a lightweight proposition in a world of heavyweight problems. Just as our backs need clothing and our stomachs need food, our souls need beauty. Beauty inspires us, fills us with joy; it attracts us to that nourishing, creative forces that resides in our hearts. The love of beauty is one of the basic qualities all humans share. If we deny that, we deny our humanness.

LYNDON B. JOHNSON'S RANCH

LYNDON B. JOHNSON'S GRAVE, LBJ RANCH

PEDERNALES RIVER, PEDERNALES FALLS STATE PARK

WILDFLOWERS AND GRASS IN KERR COUNTY

TEXAS BLUEBONNETS (*LUPINUS TEXENSIS*) IN LLANO COUNTY

WINDMILL AND WILDFLOWERS

RANCHING: MORE THAN A BUSINESS

*"Barbed wire signaled an end to the open range. What
had been an adventure became a business."*
Inscription in the museum at the Lyndon B. Johnson
National Historic Park

The Hill Country is unique among Texas ranch land. The vegetation, climate, and terrain of these rugged limestone hills can support three distinct types of grazing livestock: cattle, sheep, and goats. Cattle forage on the grass. The variety of brush and forbs, the herbaceous plants that grow among the grasses, supports sheep and goats. Cattle favor the flatter areas while sheep and goats scramble along the slopes. The dry climate assists by minimizing the problems caused by internal parasites. A fourth herbivore, the white-tailed deer, competes with the sheep and goats for food.

Any time new species, whether wild or domestic, plant or animal, enter an area, they begin to alter the ecology and eventually the physical appearance of their environment. The endless process of erosion that began carving the rugged hills after the last Cretaceous sea receded has a contemporary accomplice: modern grazing and farming practices. The effects of human occupation have done more to change the face of these ancient hills than a thousand years of erosion from wind and rain. Overgrazing and farming has stripped off the protective vegetation and allowed the soil to wash away during the torrential thunderstorms common to this rugged country.

"My Uncle Gus [Schreiner] came to the Y.O. in 1890," said Charles Schreiner III, owner of the fifty-five-thousand-acre Y.O. ranch. "He showed me a place on the ranch where he once drove his wagon and looked out across the hills. He said it was a sea of waist-deep grass then, not a tree in sight. Now it's covered with cedar. Cedar clearing costs thirty to forty dollars an acre. Do much of that and it's like buying the land all over again."

The loss of topsoil and elimination of wildfires have allowed cedar (Ashe juniper) to invade the grasslands and form dense cedar brakes. The brakes shade out grass and other vegetation that sustain livestock and wildlife. Ranchers retaliate with chain saws and draglines to eliminate the brush and restore the native grasslands. They also use goats, who eat cedar seedlings. By rotating goats from pasture to pasture, ranchers keep cedar from invading the open areas.

Ranchers gauge their land by the number of acres needed to support one animal unit. An animal unit equals either a one thousand-pound cow, six sheep, seven goats, or seven deer. Typically, one animal unit requires fifteen to thirty acres of Hill Country range. To run the numbers of livestock necessary to bring in sufficient profits to remain solvent requires thousands of acres.

Longhorns were the first livestock to feast on the verdant grasses that once covered the Hill Country. The renowned longhorn is a legacy of the Spanish conquistadors. Coronado herded the first cattle north of the Rio Grande in 1540. Within a hundred years, Spanish cattle were ranging wild throughout the brushlands of Mexico and south Texas. They had to survive disease, scorching heat, droughts, and freezing weather. Only the hardiest, fleetest, most resourceful creatures lived to produce offspring. By the 1860s, when cowboys began rounding them up to drive north, a breed of range-wise cattle had developed that Texas could call its own. The longhorn's endurance and stamina made possible the perilous trail drives destined for the future. The longhorns of yesterday and today have a survival instinct that no domestic breed can match.

In 1867, the railroad reached Kansas and opened up the eastern beef market to Texas. Samuel Johnson, Lyndon Johnson's grandfather, and Charles Schreiner, an early businessman in Kerrville, assembled large herds of free-ranging longhorns from south Texas and trailed them north. A cow purchased for $1 to $7 in Texas brought $30 to $40 at the Dodge City railhead fifteen hundred miles north. Many a rancher made his fortune during the lusty but short-lived trail drive era between 1867 and 1886. And many went bust when they couldn't sell their cattle in a glutted Kansas market. A bankrupt Samuel Johnson left his grandson Lyndon a rich heritage, but little else. Captain Charles Schreiner had a banking and mercantile business to help through the hard times, and eventually assembled a half-million-acre ranching empire, including the famous Y.O. Ranch, still the largest ranch in the Hill Country.

The craggy, intemperate longhorn captured the heart of Americans and has become forever identified with the ranching and cowboy image, but this critter disappeared from the range soon after railroads reached the Lone Star state. Herefords, with better-tasting meat and gentler disposition, replaced longhorns as the breed of choice.

Though Herefords and longhorns have historical precedence in the rocky Hill Country pastures, ranchers have never been able to survive on the profits from cattle alone. In contrast to our prototypic image of the Old West cowboy, the typical central Texas rancher of the late 1800s spoke not with a Texas drawl, but with a German accent. He herded not ornery longhorns, but docile sheep and goats. Ranchers may brag about their cattle, but sheep and goats always have been the pocketbook of Hill Country ranching. Profits from wool and mohair pull the ranchers through the tough periods when cattle prices plummet.

The Edwards Plateau is perhaps the finest angora goat country in the world. By the late 1800s, ranchers had stocked the hills of Kerr, Edwards, Real, and Bandera counties with angora goats. Charles Schreiner established huge warehouses in Kerrville, and in 1886 shipped eight million pounds of mohair. One hundred years later, central Texas still reigns as the mohair capital of the world. The Hill Country produces 97 percent of the nation's mohair and 15 percent of its wool.

IT'S NOT LIKE THE MOVIES

Hill Country ranchers have one primary asset: land that was bequeathed to them by their fathers and their fathers' fathers. It's land that is now far too expensive to buy and pay for with the slim profits from raising livestock; land that, if lost, is lost to them forever. And when ranchers lose their land, they lose their way of life, and part of the heritage disappears that made Texas, the cowboy, and the cattle drive not just an American, but a worldwide, legend.

"Ranching isn't like the image you see in the movies," Perry Bushong said with a slight grin and a toothpick in the corner of his mouth. "People have the impression of ranching as a romantic way of life. Well, it's more than a way of life. It's a business. We can't let sentiment make our decisions. Ranchers get only about 2 percent return on their money. With that kind of cash flow, you have to be a good businessman to survive today."

Perry Bushong raises sheep, goats, and cattle on his Hill Country ranch. He sat in a straight-backed chair on the glassed-in porch of his Real County home, dressed in a white shirt, blue jeans, and well broken-in boots. He recently completed a term as president of the Mohair Council of America, which took him around the world promoting Texas mohair. A small backyard of Bermuda grass bordered with snapdragons separates his homestead from his ranching operations. His grandfather's old wooden windmill, a reminder of times past, shifts lazily in the breeze behind the patio.

He looked out across the sweeping view from his modest hillside house and surveyed his ranch, the ranch he inherited, the ranch he's determined to pass on to his daughters. Pride showed in his face and in the way he talked about a rancher's life. Perry is proud of his heritage. He is proud of his land, proud of every blade of grass clinging to the rocky soil, and of every animal grazing on it.

The roots of ranching grow deeper than the grass. For Perry Bushong, they grow four generations deep. But his vision encompasses more than hindsight. With one daughter already ranching and with three grandchildren, the heritage and land he will bequeath extends two generations into the future. Understanding the vision that encompasses past and future generations is essential to understanding ranchers and the ranching tradition.

A rancher's pride may be rooted in family heritage, but it's nourished daily by a life of hard work. Everything a rancher has is the result of intense manual labor. Not labor done and finished, but labor that began when their great-grandparents drove the first stock onto virgin grasslands. Labor that hasn't abated for a single day, sunup to sundown, for four generations. Ranching affords no vacation from washed-out fences, busted water pumps, sick or injured stock, or the other scheduled or unpredictable chores.

The list of tasks required to keep a ranch operating is enough to boggle the mind and weary the body of a city-bred man like myself. Four to five times a year all the livestock have to be rounded up by horseback, a job requiring several weeks. The stock have to be counted and earmarked or branded. The sheep and goats are dipped for ticks and lice and drenched for stomach worms and the cattle sprayed to help ward off flies.

In the spring, the Bushongs herd as many sheep and goats as possible into pens for lambing and kidding. The young need all the protection they can get from predators. Later in the spring, the sheep and goats are rounded up again for shearing. Goats are sheared again in the fall.

Caring for the stock is a full-time job itself, but it's only a fraction of the work required to keep a ranch solvent. Maintenance is another full-time job, a job that is never finished. Consider fence work, pump, well, and windmill maintenance, road maintenance, weed control, equipment repair, and stock feeding. Then include keeping breeding records for registered stock, analyzing stock prices, bookkeeping, and the other aspects of running a business. This adds up to several full-time jobs.

Despite the macho Marlboro image, ranching is not exclusively a man's world. The Hill Country is replete with women who have run their own ranches, mastered the hardships, and passed their ranches intact to the next generation. Whether shouldering the responsibilities alone or sharing them with their husbands, women are as much a part of the ranching tradition as the cowboy and the longhorn. Joan Bushong invests as much day-to-day energy in running the ranch as her husband. She looks at every sheep, every goat, and every cow on her ranch with the discerning eye of someone who knows and loves the stock.

As a way of life, the basic challenges of holding a ranch together haven't changed much since sheep and goats first tasted Hill Country grass. "We have three major concerns," Joan said. She has curly blond hair and speaks with a drawl reminiscent of Lady Bird Johnson.

"We have to contend with droughts and severe cold. Nothing depresses a rancher more than drought. We don't know whether to sell stock, or to hold on and hope and pray for rain. Then there's fluctuating prices. We never know from year to year what the stock will bring. And predators are a constant problem. We have coyotes, eagles, and Russian boars. What's hard is that we have so little control over these factors."

If you want a spirited conversation, ask any rancher about predators. Joan searched for the right words. "City people don't understand that it's like someone coming into your home and stealing everything you have, not just your possessions, but robbing you of your way of life. If we can't make a profit, we lose our ranch and our entire way of life. We can't survive economically without predator control.

"In 1985, we lost practically every kid and lamb on the ranch to coyotes," Joan said.

"That's when Perry went out and bought the donkeys. They live with the goats and protect them from coyotes. They work pretty well in small pastures."

"We didn't use to have any coyote problems," Perry said. "Then the environmentalists outlawed 1080 [a poison that kills all carnivores, including foxes and other harmless species]. So we had to look for other solutions. Donkeys are just a tool. They help, but they don't solve the problem."

Y.O.'s Charles Schreiner III (Charlie Three) explained a rancher's options in simple terms. "Some people say that they just love to hear coyotes howling at dusk. So do I – in Yellowstone, but not on my ranch. I had the choice of raising goats or coyotes," he said. "We were losing 80 percent of the kids to predators, so I gave up on goats. We raise longhorns now, and a few sheep. Last year we lost 15 percent of the lambs to coyotes."

The howling of coyotes has already replaced the *baa-baa* of goats and sheep in south and west Texas, and mohair and wool ranching are declining on the Edwards Plateau. Yet coyotes are only part of the predator problem.

"The Hill Country is the ice-cream parlor for eagles in the United States," Charlie Three said. "I remember driving out to one pasture with nannies and kids and looking up and seeing fourteen bald eagles circling. Government biologists analyzed the talon marks in the carcasses and proved that the eagles were killing the kids. So they netted some of the birds and took them down to the coast. You know, it doesn't take long for an eagle to fly back here from the coast," he said with a slight smile.

When eagles came under the protection of the endangered species laws, ranchers had to abandon the practice of shotgunning the soaring raptors from small aircraft. In one year, eagles killed two thousand sheep on the Y.O., costing the ranch $40,000. Fortunately, eagles live in the Hill Country only during the winter and migrate north in the spring. Ranchers have adopted the practice of lambing after March 1 when the eagles have gone.

"By waiting so late to lamb, we miss the spring market," Joan Bushong said. "Without the spring grass, the lambs and kids don't grow as large, so sometimes they don't bring as good a price. And we have to contend with needle grass in summer. The needle grass gets in their wool and pierces their bellies. The hot weather and irritation from the grass causes them to lose weight."

After discussing the predator problem, Perry added another major concern of modern ranchers. "There's a fourth big problem ranchers have to contend with today: the environmentalists and the antihunting and animal rights groups. They're city people that are well educated, above average income, and very vocal, but they don't understand the grassroots, the nuts and bolts of ranching. They're well meaning, but the ideal situation is not always the same as the practical situation. On a ranch we have to use practical solutions. My grandfather said that there's always three sides to any problem: your side, their side, and the right side. I'm open to changing, but not until I get proof that justifies the change.

"Politics has a strong influence on ranching," Perry continued. "The voting public doesn't understand the problems of the agricultural sector, and most of the votes are in the cities. The politicians cater to the cities where they can get the votes. Ranchers have always been independent, but that's to our detriment now. Our city cousins have banded together. Now we have to band together to get enough political power to survive."

Survival. It's a word you hear ranchers use frequently. They must survive droughts, predators, price fluctuations, and adverse politics. In order to survive the fluctuating economy of the past two decades, ranching has changed in ways that would have amazed the fathers of Perry Bushong and Charlie Schreiner III.

After an absence lasting one hundred years, longhorns have returned to the Edwards Plateau. During the drought of the 1950s when no rain fell on much of the Hill Country for six years, Charlie Three had to take Y.O.'s last two hundred head of Herefords to Two Dot, Montana, to find enough grass to survive. In 1957, after the drought broke, Charlie Three stepped back in time and reintroduced longhorns to the Y.O. His herd and the interest in longhorns had grown so much by 1964 that he founded the Texas Longhorn Breeders Association. Now, he and many other ranchers raise registered longhorns to sell and to breed with Herefords. No domestic cow can thrive in this rugged country as well as the longhorn. A longhorn-Hereford calf retains many of the survival characteristics of the sire.

Another change for today's rancher is the economic importance of the white-tailed deer. Selling hunting leases is a growing source of income. Ranchers now surround their property with six-foot high, deer-proof fences to manage the wildlife on their land. So now you can add wildlife management to the expertise required for the modern rancher.

The previous generation of ranchers were accustomed to the abundant deer population, but they would be startled to see the animals that bolt through the brush today. Exotic deer and antelope now share the range with domestic stock and native wildlife. Charlie Three, once again setting the pace for Hill Country ranchers, began stocking the Y.O. with exotic game in 1953, and founded the Texas Exotic Game Association in 1965.

"Today, the Y.O. has about fifty species and seven thousand head of exotic animals, including four endangered species," said Louis Schreiner, general manager of the Y.O. and youngest of Charlie Three's four sons. "But we breed predominantly six species: axis, fallow, and sika deer, black buck antelope, and Aoudad and Corsican sheep. We raise most to sell. Hunters kill only about 2 percent a year. That's less than die of natural causes. Fifty percent of Y.O.'s income comes from exotics, and another 25 percent from tourism." Unlike other ranches, the Y.O. has motel facilities, youth camps, and a drive-through African game section with giraffes, zebras, oryx, and other exotics.

The changes in Hill Country ranching in the past decade may be only a prelude to what the future holds. "Wildlife, especially exotics, is becoming a major industry in the Hill Country," said Louis Schreiner. Though hunting is an economic boost to ranchers, the real value in exotics may come from the high quality meat they produce, while requiring little management. Ranchers are hoping that the venison market will develop in this country as it has in New Zealand. That country exports one thousand tons of venison annually.

Another trend is more predictable. Perry Bushong calls it the subdivision trend. "Most of the ranches between San Antonio and Boerne have already been subdivided," he said. "We're making more people, but we can't make more land. The subdivisions keep moving farther west."

"The recreational value of the land today is higher than the ranching value," said Louis Schreiner. "We're seeing lots of absentee landowners, now." The Y.O. is selling twelve thousand of its fifty-five thousand acres in ten- to one-hundred-acre tracts. Most buyers are from the larger Texas cities, but more and more are coming in from California and the Midwest.

So, the Hill Country is in the midst of change, a change that began one hundred fifty years ago and shows no signs of abating. The European settlers displaced the Indians, sheep and goats displaced the longhorns, cedar brakes displaced the seas of grass, springs and creeks dried up, and impounded lakes inundated the dry hills. Now, subdivisions and absentee landowners are displacing the ranchers, and the economy is shifting from livestock to tourism.

Yes, the Hill Country is changing, but as Texas folklorist J. Frank Dobie said, "A land that cannot be plowed under keeps its traditions." The city folks come to buy not just raw land, but the heritage of Hill Country. They want to buy a part of the life-style that made the cowboy a folk hero and the symbol of manliness.

The economy has changed, the plant and animal associations have changed, but the appeal of the Hill Country remains the same today as when the German settlers forded the Guadalupe, Pedernales, and Llano rivers in ox-drawn wagons. Today's settlers come in Fords, Toyotas, and BMWs, but they are looking for the same elusive but integral ingredient of life: space. Not empty space, but space filled with vistas that nourish the spirit, space filled with the scent of freshness and the soothing sounds of nature, space filled with the opportunity to experience a new and challenging life-style.

Will the economic swing from livestock to tourism, from ranches to subdivisions, eventually cause the demise of the ranching way of life? Ranchers have always been survivors. They still consider their heritage as valuable an asset as their land. They will hold on as long as there is a market for cattle, wool, and mohair. And if that falters, they will look for alternatives, such as wildlife and exotic game. Some are even growing grapes and producing wine that rivals the best vintages of California. Ranching may look different in the future, but the ranching heritage will continue to thrive in the rugged hills of central Texas. It's more than a business, it's a way of life.

AN OLD RANCH HOUSE IN REAL COUNTY

SHEEP AND LAMBS IN REAL COUNTY

GALLAGER RANCH IN BEXAR COUNTY

"EXOTIC" ANIMALS AT THE Y.O. RANCH

LONGHORN AT THE Y.O. RANCH

ENCHANTED ROCK STATE NATURAL AREA

A HILL COUNTRY BANQUET OF PARKS

*"When we require of a beautiful object only that it be
itself, we find beauty everywhere.... the
proper treatment of something that rewards us simply by
being itself is to permit it to remain itself,
interfering with it as little as possible."*
Alexander F. Skutch, Life Ascending

The Hill Country, with all its beauty and ruggedness, is privately owned and inaccessible to the public, except for a series of state parks. Like a smorgasbord, each park offers a slightly different flavor of this country that so stimulates our appetite for the outdoors. Twelve parks round out the menu.

For the historic hors d'oeuvres, you'll want to visit the state and national historical parks honoring Lyndon B. Johnson. In Johnson City you can see the president's boyhood home and the reconstructed Johnson settlement with a herd of longhorns, the log house of Sam Ealy Johnson (Lyndon's grandfather), stone barns, and an exhibit center depicting the legendary era of the trail drive. At the LBJ state park and ranch, you can taste (sometimes literally) life in the 1800s at the Saur-Beckmann living historic farm. Workers maintain the farm and house in the traditional life-style, including hardy meals with homemade bread, fresh garden vegetables, and canned goods. A bus takes visitors on a tour of the LBJ ranch, birthplace, and cemetery.

For appetizers of the nature of the Hill Country, you can visit Kerrville State Park, located on the southern outskirts of that city. It stretches along the shaded banks of the Guadalupe River and into the surrounding hills. Swimming and tubing are the main attractions. If you desire more of a taste of the rugged hills, a series of loop trails lead through woodlands of juniper and oak. Besides its swimming areas, the park's outstanding feature is the large numbers of white-tailed deer that graze the roadsides and camping areas at dusk.

Swimming and wildlife are also the main attractions at Guadalupe River State Park, north of San Antonio. The river winds around scenic limestone bluffs and through a series of rapids before Canyon Lake captures it downstream from the park.

The cypress-lined banks of the Frio River at Garner State Park are guaranteed to whet your appetite for the Hill Country. Tubers basted with suntan lotion lie back and let the spring-fed river whisk them over cascades, around boulders, and through slow channels of deep water. This popular recreational spot has cabins, screened shelters, and 350 campsites.

If a recreational menu is your bill of fare, Inks Lake State Park offers a potluck of activities. The sandy shoreline and picturesque coves of the lake provide boating, fishing, swimming, and other water-oriented activities. You can hike and explore the weathered outcroppings of colorful granite and metamorphic rocks. In the spring, wildflowers decorate the park like a picnic blanket spread across the hillsides. A nine-hole golf course awaits those with an appetite for golf. You can sample the underground beauty of the Hill Country in nearby Longhorn Caverns State Park.

Colorado Bend State Park, on the northern edge of the Hill Country near Lampasas, preserves 5,328 acres of scenery, an undeveloped cave, one of the most impressive waterfalls in the state, and a beautiful section of the Colorado River before it flows into Lake Buchanan. Because of their delicate ecology, the waterfalls and cave are closed until a master plan is developed for the park.

When you're ready for a main course of classic Hill Country, au naturel, your selection of entrees includes Pedernales Falls State Park, Hill Country State Natural Area, and Honey Creek State Natural Area. At Pedernales Falls State Park east of Johnson City, the Pedernales River creates a series of cascades and serpentine channels in the exposed bedrock. The power of eons of flash floods is evident in the sculpted and polished boulders, including one lodged in a crevice high on a cliff side.

By hiking up the streams and tributaries of the river, you can discover secret places with delicate beauty. Fern-covered waterfalls, creek beds with bathtub-like holes, and rare plants lay hidden among the juniper-covered hills like select vintage bottles of wine in a crowded cellar. Hikers and backpackers can enjoy a seven-mile loop trail that traverses the hills and drainages to the more remote reaches of the river.

Honey Creek State Natural Area is another entree on the Hill Country menu. This delicate area is open by tour only from the Guadalupe River State Park. It encompasses meadows and a beautiful creek with palmettos, bald cypress, and water so pure the early settlers considered it as sweet as honey.

The Hill Country State Natural Area west of Bandera was until recently a working ranch. Now it is a favorite place for hikers and horseback riders. A six-mile loop trail leads to a primitive camping area. Side trails ascend the hilltops for scenic views of the countryside. Years of cedar clearing have removed most of the junipers typical of the area, but the other trees and shrubs remain relatively undisturbed. (Note: The park has no facilities and is closed to the public from 5 P.M. Monday until 8 A.M. Wednesday morning.)

No Hill Country gourmet would consider a repast complete without sampling the house specialties: Enchanted Rock and Lost Maples state natural areas. Here you will find the Hill Country at its finest. Enchanted Rock offers a daring specialty: rock climbing. The steep slopes of the granite dome attract novice and expert climbers alike. Numerous routes with various levels of difficulty have been mapped along the cracks and ridges of the precipitous walls.

If you prefer not to dangle above open spaces, you can enjoy the spectacular views by hiking to the summit of the windswept mountain. The eroding forces of wind and rain have sculpted the rocky slopes with minature valleys, potholes, and a deep crack cave. Gnarled live oaks, prickly pear cacti, and blankets of wildflowers sink their roots in the soil collected in cracks and shallow depressions. A hiking and backpacking trail circles the mammoth dome and the adjacent smaller dome. Explorers will delight in the fern and claret cup cacti and the colorful lichen that decorate the sometimes bizarre shapes of the eroded rocks. Deer and armadillos are frequent guests, especially near dusk.

Lost Maples has a specialty rare in the woodlands of Texas—autumn color. The Sabinal River canyon and the creeks flowing into it harbor a population of bigtooth maple trees. Like their eastern counterparts, these small-leaved maples turn spectacular shades of red, yellow, and orange in the fall. But Lost Maples offers more than a once-a-year banquet. The verdant canyons with spring-fed streams greet spring with as much beauty as the fall extraganza. You can sample the scenic vistas along ten miles of trails that wind along the wooded creeks and over rocky ridges. The trail system incorporates a variety of loops varying from easy to moderately strenuous hikes.

Like a consummate restaurant, the Hill Country parks offer something for everyone. From a light fare of swimming and picnicking to a heavy course of backpacking to remote areas, the parks await your pleasure. But be warned: this is one diet that could be habit-forming. For the Hill Country nourishes a basic human appetite, the need of our creative self to commune with the creative force in nature.

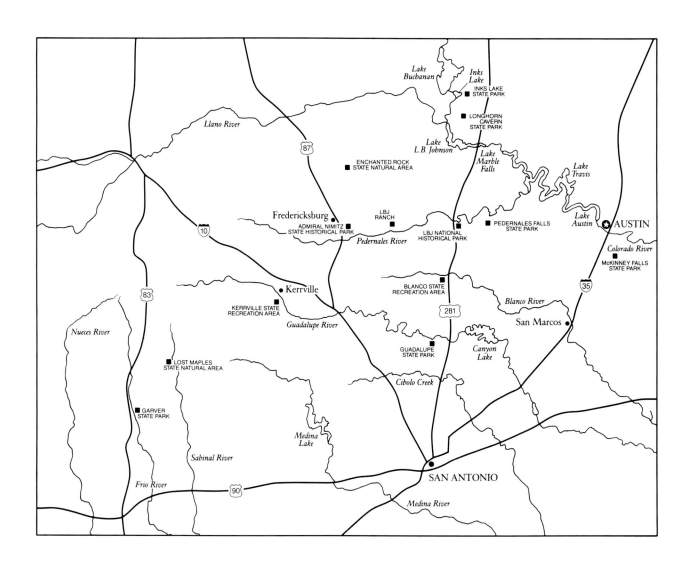

Lake
Buchanan

Inks
Lake

■ INKS LAKE
STATE PARK

■ LONGHORN
CAVERN
STATE PARK

Llano River

87

Lake
L.B. Johnson

Lake
Marble
Falls

Lake
Travis

ENCHANTED ROCK
STATE NATURAL AREA ■

10

Fredericksburg ●

LBJ
RANCH ■

■ ADMIRAL NIMITZ
STATE HISTORICAL PARK

Pedernales River

LBJ NATIONAL
HISTORICAL PARK ■

■ PEDERNALES FALLS
STATE PARK

Lake
Austin

☆ AUSTIN

Colorado River

McKINNEY FALLS
STATE PARK

35

83

● Kerrville

■ BLANCO STATE
RECREATION AREA

■ KERRVILLE STATE
RECREATION AREA

Guadalupe River

281

Blanco River

San Marcos ●

Nueces River

■ LOST MAPLES
STATE NATURAL AREA

■ GUADALUPE
STATE PARK

Canyon
Lake

Cibolo Creek

■ GARVER
STATE PARK

Medina
Lake

Sabinal River

SAN ANTONIO ●

Frio River

90

Medina River

LOST MAPLES STATE NATURAL AREA

MCKINNEY FALLS ON ONION CREEK,
MCKINNEY FALLS STATE PARK

GORMAN FALLS, COLORADO BEND STATE PARK

ABOUT THE AUTHOR

George Oxford Miller is an environmental photojournalist who has written several books about Texas including *Texas Parks and Campgrounds*, *Texas Photo Safaris*, *A Field Guide to Wildflowers, Trees and Shrubs of Texas*, and his most recent book, also published by Voyageur Press, *Landscaping with Native Plants of Texas and the Southwest*.

Miller is past co-president of the San Marcos chapter of the Native Plant Society and has taught several courses in plant studies and landscaping. A former weekly columnist for the *Austin American Statesman*, he has published articles in such publications as *Texas Highways*, *Mother Earth News*, *Texas Gardener*, *Sierra*, *Texas Parks & Wildlife*, and *National Parks Magazine*.

NEW LEAVES AND DEVELOPING SEEDS OF A
BIGTOOTH MAPLE (*ACER GRANDIDENTATUM*)